'A fine new talent' *Evening Standard*

Serving it Up
'Combines a promising talent for sparky, funny dialogue with a bleak vision of racism and rage in London's East End ... What is astonishing is that it manages to be rancidly funny and deeply chilling at the same time.' *Guardian*

A Week with Tony
'In his new play [Eldridge] shifts his attention further up the social scale with a wily look at the Conservative middle classes as they brace themselves for a likely Labour election victory.' *Independent*

David Eldridge was born in 1973 in Romford where he still lives. In February 1996 the Bush Theatre premiered his first full-length play, *Serving it Up*, the second work in the Time Out award-winning London Fragments' season. In June 1996, the Steam Industry produced his second play, *A Week with Tony*, at the Finborough Theatre. He has also had two short plays produced: *Cabbage for Tea, Tea, Tea!* (University of Exeter/Platform Four) and *Dirty* (Theatre Royal Stratford East Young Voices/The NAYT Big Youth Theatre Festival). Following an eight-week attachment to the Royal National Theatre Studio in spring 1996, he completed his third play, *Summer Begins* (Donmar Warehouse, March 1997). David's first screenplay, *The Tall Boy*, is being developed by Tapson Steel Films and British Screen. He is currently writer in residence at the Royal National Theatre Studio under the Pearson Television Theatre Writers' Scheme and is under commission from the Bush Theatre and Soho Theatre Company.

Methuen Modern Plays

First published in Great Britain in 1997
by Methuen
Random House, 20 Vauxhall Bridge Road, London
SW1V 2SA
and Random House Australia (Pty) Limited, 20 Alfred
Street, Milsons Point, Sydney, New South Wales 2061,
Australia
Random House New Zealand Limited, 18 Poland Road,
Glenfield, Auckland 10, New Zealand
Random House South Africa (Pty) Limited, Endulini,
5A Jubilee Road, Parktown 2193, South Africa

Serving it Up first published by the Bush Theatre in 1996
copyright © 1996, 1997 by David Eldridge
A Week with Tony copyright © 1997 by David Eldridge
Introduction copyright © 1997 David Eldridge

The author has asserted his moral rights

ISBN 0 413 71340 7

A CIP catalogue record for this book is available
from the British Library

Typeset by Wilmaset Ltd, Birkenhead, Wirral
Printed and bound by Cox & Wyman Ltd, Reading,
Berkshire

David Eldridge

Serving it Up
&
A Week with Tony

WITHDRAWN

Methuen Drama

Contents

Introduction

I can remember as a teenager arriving from school to the stall where I worked in Romford Market. The first thing I did was to get in the big trailer, which occupied half the pitch, packed wall-to-wall with the stock of ladies' shoes, and change quickly out of my school uniform into the familiar dirty baggy jeans all the other market boys wore. I didn't go to school locally as I had an assisted place (funded by Havering council) and part-scholarship to attend an independent school six or seven miles away. I used to hate that gross grey tweed uniform. I used to think everyone was looking at me when I got on the bus at Romford station, and on non-market days, I don't think there was one journey home, wearing those disgusting grey tweeds, when the thought of being beaten up by some local schoolboys didn't cross my mind. Growing up, I often felt I lived a double life. An averagely surly market boy in Romford, and a quietish bloke who played football at the posh school, and, for a while as a sixth-former, went to some ballroom dancing sessions, with the all-girls' school down the road. Although I would have pleaded my only interest was in the girls (honest), I suspect if the market boys had ever found that out, I'd have never lived it down!

When people, who don't know me, have asked me about these plays there's often surprise that these first two plays should be so different. In the same way other students at Exeter University found it hard to believe the bloke with the thick Essex accent was 'public school', I guess after *Serving it Up*, others were surprised I'd written about London and Home Counties middle classes. 'Can this *Trainspotting*-generation-East-Ender really write about the Conservative classes?' you can feel the questions implying. But, although these two plays propose two very different portraits of modern Britain, they both grow out of the same life experience, and, on reflection, I think, both grow out of a feeling of anger at the frustrated aspirations of those living in the south-east.

At university, I was very angry that those living in east London's deprived council estates scarcely find their voices heard in Britain today. As society closes its eyes, covers its ears and turns its back, all we have are filtered images on television screens and fragmented memories of the last time we strayed from our safe homes. It chokes me to think of Sonny as a small boy, rattling around Hackney's glass-littered playgrounds with a cricket bat. I suspect, if Sonny still has a cricket bat now, it's for use as a weapon, and that's sad. For me this play is as much about disaffected middle age as youth and it always saddened me when audiences laughed at Charlie's fall at the end of Act One, and Val stuffing her face with cake at the end. Far easier, in the great tradition of British theatre, to laugh at 'the working classes', than admit and demonstrate an emotional point of contact.

I was deeply angry, too, observing how the pain of the recession had affected families of those attending my school and outside, who had struggled to build businesses their whole lives. All around them, however, other people I knew and saw were carrying on as if nothing else was happening in the country. I can remember actually overhearing an Exeter Young Conservative remarking that he thought there weren't really any poor people any more. I always loved Trevor Griffiths' notion of a 'Tory Story', and linking this with an interest in politics, some anger and empathy with the Tory classes and the opportunity a commission from the Steam Industry provided to write a large cast play, *A Week with Tony* was born.

For me, both *Serving it Up* and *A Week with Tony* are attempts to understand what has made their central characters the people they are. Sonny is seen in relation to his best mate, girlfriends, mum and dad, and the past when his cricket-playing friend, Ryan, returns to the East End. What's made Sonny the sort of man who can slash a face at a bus stop – who can eventually do the same to his best friend? Tony is seen in relation to his former life with his wife, daughter and the Tory Party, and in relation to his new partner and his new job. Why does Tony chase the dream of making his daughter's wedding plans a reality – why can't he let go of the past? These plays may not be 'brothers', but they're very closely related. The dramaturgy may be different – rough hewn slices of life form *Serving it Up* and a conventional 'big' structure for *A Week with Tony* – but these plays are blood relatives.

Thanks to all those who have encouraged me in the process of writing these first plays – especially: Peter Thomson, James MacDonald, Jackie Tinsley, Alex Cross, Ruth Prior, Emma Pallant, Philip Skinner, Paul Sirett, Mark Ravenhill, Lin Coghlan, Phil Wilmott, Louise Mulvey, Ali Robertson, Ben Jancovich, Rob West, Joanne Reardon, Dominic Dromgoole and last, but definitely not least, my brilliant agent, Alan.

Thank you too, to Michael Willis from Brentwood and Ongar Conservative Association, who helped me research *A Week with Tony*, and read drafts, and those from Enfield Conservative Association who kindly attended some early rehearsals.

David Eldridge, January 1997

Serving it Up

*for my dad
and Trevor
and the Romford Market boys, 1986–1992*

Serving it Up was first performed at the Bush Theatre, London, on 14 February 1996. The cast was as follows:

Teresa	Kacey Ainsworth
Ben/Ryan	James Bannon
Charlie	Christopher Ettridge
Val	Arbel Jones
Sonny	Eddie Marsan
Wendy	Melissa Wilson
Nick	Jake Wood

Directed by Jonathan Lloyd
Designed by Nick Sargent
Lighting by Paul Russell
Sound by Seb Lee-Delisle

Characters

Sonny
Nick
Val
Charlie
Wendy
Teresa
Ben *and* **Ryan**
(*who should be played by the same actor*)

Setting

1990s east London.

'Serving up' is a slang term for drug-dealing in parts of east London.

Act One

Scene One

A park bench somewhere in east London. **Sonny** *is a skinhead. Both boys are hard-faced and look out at the audience most of the time.*

Nick It's the environment.

Sonny Do what?

Nick Environment, we did it at school, didn't we?

Sonny Mr Swindler?

Nick Yeah, that's right.

Sonny He was a tit.

Nick I liked him. He told jokes.

Sonny Went on about whales all the time.

Nick He wasn't from Wales?

Sonny No. Whales – the big fish in the sea, you turd. Had a Save The Planet badge.

Nick I reckon they've got to do something about the environment.

Sonny What?

Nick The sun will burn the shit out of us.

Sonny Load of bollocks put about by the government. Give us a fag.

Nick That salmon you are going to light up is contributing to the ozone.

Sonny Will you shut up? Haven't you got anything better to say? What about the bird down at the chip shop?

Nick Piss off.

Sonny Big knockers.

Nick   Leave it out.

Sonny   Good shag?

Nick   I didn't shag her.

Sonny   Bullshit!

Nick   Wouldn't let me do it.

Sonny   No way!

Nick   Didn't have a wet suit, did I? Gave me a blow job though.

Sonny   You should've put her in her place. You could have shot it all over her stomach.

Nick   She might've had a dose of crabs.

Sonny   Got a right fit mum she has. Wouldn't mind fucking a mum, eh, Nicky-boy? Nice old piece of roughage to teach you a lesson or two.

Nick   Yeah.

Sonny   Know something about her sister an' all.

Nick   Oh yeah?

Sonny   Got Aids.

Nick   No way!

Sonny   Straight up. HGV positive, mate. Wears one of them red ribbons an' all.

Nick   I'm not going to that chip shop any more. You know I've had saveloy and chips every week for the last year. I thought it had started to smell funny. Must've been contaminated.

Sonny   Have to get a blood test now.

They laugh. Silence.

Nick   Picking up my motor tomorrow, Sonny. Lovely. Escort mark two. Red it is. Some rust on the doors and wheel-arches but it's superb. Danny's old man reckons I'll get ninety out of it.

Sonny   Ninety my arse. Where? Downhill?

Nick   No, it's proper.

Sonny   Boy-racer now, Nicky-boy. Down on the circuit. On the front at Southend?

Nick   We'll go to the countryside.

Sonny   Yeah, Kent.

Nick   Yeah, do a couple of pills and drive. We'll fly. Excellent.

Sonny   Kent. (*A beat.*) My dad's always going on about Kent. He used to go hopping when he was a kid.

Nick   Hopping?

Sonny   Picking hops, to make beer. They used to do it in the old days, before tractors. My dad used to go in the summer.

Nick   Sounds really shit to me.

Sonny   I reckon they had a real laugh. Sleeping out. Rabbiting and all that. My dad reckons he did his cherry hopping. Said her fanny smelt soapy. The old git still thinks he's Tom Jones.

Nick   I like your dad.

Sonny   You don't have to live with him.

Nick   He's all right.

Sonny   He gets right on my tits.

Nick   First time I got pissed, in the pub with your dad and you. Mine wouldn't drink with me. Wanker.

Pause. **Sonny** *notices something in the distance and smiles.*

Sonny   Oi, Nick, look at that, look at that! Oi – get your tits out!

Pause. **Nick** *laughs.*

Same to you an' all!

Sonny *gestures with two fingers.*

Nick   You're knocked.

Pause.

Sonny   Nick.

Nick   What?

Sonny   Remember your birthday?

Nick   What a night.

Sonny   It was brilliant.

Nick   The pub was packed . . .

Sonny   I was fucked on gear and drink, I puked out of me arse.

Nick   What? You shit yourself?

Sonny   No – it was puke. Brilliant night, Nicky-boy. I fucked Vikki that night. Cunt like a Big Mac.

Pause.

I wouldn't mind a regular bird as it goes, Nicky-boy.

Nick   You!

Sonny   Yeah, me. I know how to show a girl a good time.

Nick   The last bird you took out threw her kebab on your head.

Sonny   Her way of saying she loved me.

Nick   Chilli sauce an' all.

Sonny   Didn't half sting.

Nick   You'd just asked her if she took it up the arse.

Sonny   Bullshit. No, not me.

Pause.

I reckon Wendy would be a good lass to take out.

Nick   She's fit.

Sonny   Not just that. She's got a bit of noddle. I like Wendy.

Nick   Known her a few years, ain't you?

Sonny   Since we were kids.

Pause.

Nick   I've been thinking about some mad stuff lately. When I'm bored, I just think about – space, Sonny.

Sonny   Space?

Nick   I've been reading a book.

Sonny   You nob.

Nick   It's not posh. No long words.

Sonny   Words bollocks. Didn't you have enough of books at school?

Nick   It's about a geezer who's pissed off. Everyone he knows walks all over him. His bird, the blokes at work, his mates . . . Well, he gets up one morning and kills them. Kills them all, takes a machine-gun to work and blows them away.

Sonny   Sounds all right.

Nick   It is.

Sonny   Is it out on video?

Nick   No. I've been thinking about loads lately. I've got itchy feet.

Sonny   You want to go to a chirpodist.

Nick   I want to do something.

Sonny   You going funny?

Nick   No, I just . . . I just get fucked off sometimes, Sonny. I get up in the morning and I walk about . . . I want something to do . . .

Sonny   Stay in bed, you tit . . .

Nick   I can't . . . I need to do something, Sonny.

Pause.

Chirpodist? Chiropodist, you plonker. Didn't anyone teach you anything?

Sonny *thinks about it.*

Sonny   No.

Pause.

Nick   This environment is heavy shit. The ice-poles melting and the ozone is bad news.

Sonny   Skin up, Nicky-boy.

Nick   I haven't got any.

Sonny   Where did you get all this environment shit?

Nick   On the telly, in the morning, *Open University.*

Sonny   What were you watching that shit for?

Nick   I was tripping. The programme really freaked me out. I thought the sun was going to explode. We'll be in the shit, Sonny. The whole world will be flooded. The bits still in the sun will fry, the ultraviolet there, Sonny.

Sonny   What?

Nick   The blue stuff coming out of sunbeds.

Sonny   Oh right! I know. It makes everything glow in the dark.

Nick   That's the one. That stuff is in the sun.

Sonny   Good on a trip that blue stuff.

Nick   Right.

Sonny   How come's the sun ain't blue?

Nick   Don't know.

Sonny   You've got all the mouth.

Nick   Well, it's not blue – it's fucking orange! (*A beat.*) That stuff though, it fucks your skin.

Sonny   They've been saying that for years. Listen, I've been to Majorca, mate, and there's nothing wrong with me.

Nick   When did you go again?

Sonny   Last year – I went last year, didn't I? Got the job to pay for it, an' all.

Nick   I've never been abroad.

Sonny   It was brilliant. On the piss every night, loads of birds, the sun and the sea. Had a couple of good rumbles an' all with the spics. Joined up with some geordies and beat the shit out of them. Got a great tan!

Nick   Did you use cream?

Sonny   Queers use cream.

Nick   You need the cream. What was I saying about the environment?

Sonny   Cream bollocks!

Nick   That ozone blocks out some of the shit in the sun, that you get cancer from. My mum says that only the darkies will survive on account of their skin being used to it all.

Sonny   No!

Nick   If we don't turn Sambo, we're dead.

Sonny   Sod that, I've been smoking since I was twelve. Already booked my appointment with the big 'C', Nicky-boy. Forty, I'm kicking the bucket.

Nick   You're not going to die then.

Sonny   Yes I am. I've planned it since I was ten. In a pub. A fight. I do this bloke over with a pool cue, fuck him right up. Just as I walk away, his mate says something, I turn, a gun. The cunt shoots me . . . in the stomach. The prick. Second bullet right between the eyes, no mistake that time, just like the Krays.

Nick   You might not last that long. You watch, a great big coon's going to cut your throat.

Sonny   How are you dying, Nick?

Nick   Nothing as good as that. I'm at home on my bed having a wank. There's a siren, it's the Russians, thousands of nukes five minutes away. They've had enough of McDonalds and Pizza Hut.

Pause.

Fuck them all, I just hope I come in time.

Sonny *laughs.*

Scene Two

A flat somewhere in east London. **Sonny**'s *parents,* **Val** *and* **Charlie**, *are sitting on the sofa. There's also an armchair.* **Charlie** *reads the* Sun *and* **Val** *knits.*

Val   Do you want some cake? I've got victoria sponge.

Charlie   I don't like it.

Val   You always used to like it.

Charlie   I didn't.

Val   I always used to make it specially.

Charlie   No you didn't.

He puts down his paper.

Val   I did. I made it listening to Tony Blackburn.

Charlie   That's it.

Val   What?

Charlie   I liked it when you made it. Now you buy it – out of a packet. I don't like it out of a packet.

Val   If I make it tomorrow will you eat it?

Charlie   I will if you put cream in it. Extra cream and I'll eat it.

Val   I'll buy some after work.

Charlie *returns to the paper. Pause. He looks up again.*

Charlie Will you put some flake on top?

Val Chocolate on a victoria sponge? That's a bit queer.

Charlie No it's not. I like it. Put chocolate on it.

He returns to the paper.

Val Viv's baby's due.

Pause.

Be nice to hear the sound of a baby in the flat again. Remember when Sonny was a baby, Charlie? He was a lovely kid.

Charlie *looks up.*

Charlie No he wasn't. He was bloody awful.

Val Not our Sonny.

Charlie Up all night screaming. (*A beat.*) I knew he was a wrong'un when he first spoke. Did he say mum or dad? No, not our Sonny. Tit! – That was his first word.

Val That was your sodding fault!

Charlie I haven't got any tits! And you were the one here all day with him. I was at work.

Val Work! You must be joking. When Sonny was born you were in Mile End Road knocking out a suitcase full of watches.

Charlie It fed us, Val, it fed us.

Val Get out of it! You're a lazy bugger. Look at you. You haven't moved in the last two hours.

Charlie I'm studying the form.

Val Pity you don't study those rebate forms.

Charlie Leave off, Val.

Pause. **Charlie** *looks at the paper.*

Val Are you going over the track later?

Charlie I might.

Pause.

Val   Sonny was a lovely kid. I had high hopes for Sonny. Could've been anything that boy, anything he wanted. If only he'd stayed on at school. Didn't I tell him, Charlie. He got off to a good start with me. He had everything he wanted.

Charlie (*finally folding his paper*)   You spoilt him, that's what. What he needed was discipline. Show 'em your strap – that's what my father always said.

Val   You can't treat children like that. You have to teach them, and talk to them . . .

Charlie   Rubbish. Round here? Get off. People from round here only go one way – down. It's all about keeping your head above water, getting one bastard before he gets you. I tried to make the boy a bit streetwise. Some lookout.

Val   Streetwise? Is that all you wanted for our boy?

Charlie   I had ideas for him all right. He could've been a great footballer, but he wanted to play cricket. Cricket! Who ever heard of a cricketer from Hackney! He could've been over at Upton Park by now. Gets my goat it does, Val.

Long pause. **Charlie** *again returns to his paper.* **Val** *lifts her knitting.*

What do you think of this pink?

Charlie *mumbles.*

Val   I like this pink. They're going to call it Alexandria.

Charlie (*looking up*)   How does Viv know it's a girl?

Val   She had a scan. I told you before. They put jelly all over her belly.

Charlie   What flavour?

Val   No, not that jelly.

Charlie   I'm pulling your leg – I'm pulling your leg!

Pause.

Alexandria – what sort of a name is that?

Val It's nice, a bit sophisticated. It's time we had something sophisticated in this family.

Charlie Was it John's idea?

Val I think so.

Charlie Bloody ponce.

Val He's all right.

Charlie Looks down his ruddy great nose at us. Your Viv hasn't been the same since she shacked up with him.

Val You can't blame her for doing better for herself. John's all right.

Charlie He's a ponce – And if he wasn't seeing your Viv I'd swear he was a bandit.

Val Never! He's been good to us. He offered Sonny a job. You heard him, Charlie.

Charlie Exactly . . .

Val All Sonny had to do was a year at college, and there it was for him. Eight thousand a year as well.

Charlie Sonny's got enough money.

Val Computers are the future, Charlie.

Charlie Gets on my wick. People like John ponce about in the city, taking us all for a ride, fiddling millions and I'm the one who gets done for having a few quid off the social!

Val It's your bloody fault. You better just hope they don't start following you over the dogs. No wonder Sonny's turned out like he has.

Charlie He's all right.

Val But where does he get his money? He doesn't work. He's going to end up in prison just like you are.

Pause.

Charlie Where is Sonny?

Val He's out with Nick.

Charlie   Good boy that Nick.

Val   He is a nice boy.

Charlie *turns again to his paper.*

Val   Nick is a nice boy. Came round this morning for a cup of tea. Ever so polite, Charlie. Made the tea as well. Makes a lovely cup of tea. Had a big slice of victoria sponge an' all.

Val *continues with her knitting. Pause.*

Charlie   Did you screw him, Val?

Val   Charlie! I wouldn't! You know I wouldn't!

Charlie   What you said before.

Val   When. When, Charlie?

Charlie *puts down his paper.*

Charlie   You know who, Sonny's mate – the boy from cricket.

Val   Never!

Charlie   You know who I mean.

Val   No!

Charlie   Don't insult me, Val! Pretty boy, bit older than Sonny. The boy who run the cricket team. What's-his-name – Ryan. That's it, Ryan . . .

Val   Once, I did it once.

Pause.

Why did you say it, Charlie! Why! You know I don't . . .

Charlie   What? Fuck boys! No, course you don't, Val. Course you don't. You just stay away from Sonny's mates. You just leave Sonny alone . . .

Val   How dare you, Charlie!

Charlie   Don't worry, Val, I don't think you fucked your own son, but just let him get on . . .

Val   What are you saying?

Charlie You know what I'm saying . . . The pissing boy can't move without you asking where he's going. Everything anyone does you have to have your two penn'orth! It's like being watched – you can't move – you smother him, like you try to smother me!

Val Smother you? – You, you're never here . . .

Charlie Oh, leave it out . . .

Val You set up home, fifteen year ago in that bloody pub. How dare you lecture me on being a mother! Hark at you mister-fucking-wonderful. The dad who changed all Sonny's nappies, who always got up in the night, who always sat down and helped him read! Father! Father, Christ, it's a fucking joke!

Charlie Val!

Val Where were you when I give birth? Twelve pissing hours I was in labour and you –

Charlie Val!

Val And when my mother died. I had Sonny, he was a baby, and you? Where the fucking hell were you, eh super-dad? Eh? – My husband. At the dogs! At the pissing dogs. You couldn't even get yourself home from the dogs when me mother was lying dead in her bed! How dare you say I smother you!

Charlie Shut up! Just shut up, just shut up, just shut up!

Pause.

You just keep quiet about your stupid poxy men and I don't give a monkey's, all right! You just make the dinner and bake the fucking cake. That's how it is.

Pause.

Scene Three

Wendy *and* **Teresa** *sit on the park bench where we saw* **Sonny** *and* **Nick** *earlier. They both smoke.*

Wendy   I've given up on a real tan. (*A beat.*) I've got to get on me mum's sunbed, Trese.

Teresa   You don't need it. Sunbed just gives you wrinkles.

Wendy   White legs. Look at them, Trese – like a milk bottle!

Teresa   Get some tanning lotion.

Wendy   It goes all streaky.

Teresa   Your legs are all right.

Wendy   This country. Sun – we've had sun all summer and the week I'm off for a weekend on the beach it's been pissing down. (*A beat.*) Mary's not coming any more. Fucking bitch. She's not getting her deposit back.

Teresa   What are you going to do?

Wendy   Well, you're not doing anything this weekend.

Teresa   I can't afford it, Wend.

Wendy   Come on – what do you reckon?

Teresa   I don't know.

Wendy   It'll be a laugh.

Teresa   A caravan in Bognor?

Wendy   You're just a snob.

Teresa   I'm not. I just draw the line at Bognor, that's all.

A beat.

Wendy   Well, if you're not going to go I'll just have to pull tonight.

Teresa   Where are we going?

Wendy   Don't know.

Teresa   I'm not going to the Red Fox again.

Wendy   Options?

Teresa   I'd rather get food poisoning at the Red Fox.

Wendy   They've changed the music now, Trese . . .

Teresa My idea of a night out does not involve five hundred sixteen-year-olds bobbing up and down on their first fucking E.

Wendy They don't play hardcore any more.

Teresa What is it? Load of metallers and a trip-head shagging a weirdo in the corner?

Wendy I thought you liked Indie?

Teresa Will you just leave it, Wend.

Wendy Sorry!

Teresa Look, there is more to life than a Friday night and a weekend in Bognor, right.

Wendy Why don't you just leave the PMT routine, Trese.

Pause.

Teresa I'm a week late.

Wendy I thought you stopped seeing Freddie?

Teresa Yeah – well.

Wendy Forget it, darling. Talk to me about it in a week's time and you'll wonder what you were worrying about. (*A beat.*) Tell you what. Wouldn't mind a dirty weekend with that Nick.

Teresa You're a nympho!

They laugh.

Nick's all right. His mate Sonny's a prat though.

Pause.

Wendy I used to fancy Sonny.

Teresa He looks like an ape.

Wendy He's not that bad.

Teresa Sonny's just like the other blokes round here. If you want to meet someone decent you've got to look up west.

Wendy I haven't got West End money.

Teresa   And most of them are wankers. I met this city bloke once, Wend. Honestly – he stroked his mobile like it was his prick. And I said to him – I don't care where you're from or how much money you've got, if you try and touch my tits again I'll knee you in the bollocks –

Pause.

I don't know why you bother with blokes so much.

Wendy   You're just a feminist.

Teresa   I'm not a feminist!

Wendy   You are! Always saying it about men. Next thing you'll be shaving your head and shagging a lesbo.

Teresa   Bloody cheek. I just don't let blokes take liberties with me.

Wendy   I like a bloke who takes a few liberties. At least it's a bit of excitement.

Teresa   It's not. They crap all over you. I'm not getting married.

Wendy (*nodding somewhere in the audience*)   Look at him over there walking his dog. I bet he ain't a piss-taker.

Teresa   He must be thirty-odd.

Wendy   I wouldn't mind an older man. Someone to look out for you. Someone to listen to, talk to.

Teresa   No. Look at his face. I've seen that look before. My dad had it. I bet he's just been with a bird, and not his wife either . . .

Wendy   No! Not him – he looks like Richard Gere.

Teresa   He's a shit – just like the rest.

Wendy   He's lovely in *Pretty Woman*. Anyway, Cindy Crawford wouldn't go with a bastard.

Teresa   They split up, you silly tart.

Pause.

Wendy   What will you do then? You can't live on your own . . .

Teresa   I'm not going to live under the thumb.

Wendy   What about when you fall in love?

Teresa   No way!

Wendy   I believe in love.

Teresa   You still believe in Father Christmas.

Pause.

It's all rubbish, Wend. You'll wake up one morning and think – I'm forty, I'm fourteen stone and I don't know what I'm doing. But before it pisses you off, you look at your old man and you ask him for a cuddle. What does he do? He rolls over, farts, and tells you to go and make him a cup of tea. I don't want that.

Wendy   You've got to have love. You've got to have love, Teresa.

Pause.

I've been in love – I know what it's like. I was in love with Jason.

Teresa   Jason?

Teresa *laughs.*

Wendy   Yes.

Teresa   That plonker? You could hit him with a hammer and that fuckwit would still grin.

Wendy   He had a nice smile.

Teresa   He was born with that. His mum dropped him on his head.

Wendy   Don't take the piss.

Teresa   And he had a twitch. We used to call him Shakin' Stevens at school!

Wendy   You always take the piss.

Teresa   Bloody hell. That's your romance? What was that? Hand up your skirt and make your fanny wet?

Wendy   Fuck off.

Teresa   Wend . . .

Wendy *goes to leave.*

Teresa   No, wait. Wait. Please, Wendy.

Wendy *stops and turns.*

Teresa   You know what I believe, Wend? Sometimes I can see it when I'm here at the park. I look at the kids with their mums and dads, and I know that I shouldn't feel it, because I look at the faces of the mums and they're so heavy and drawn – But I look at the kids and there I see it – life.

Pause.

This place, the park, the playground – You remember Wend, when we were kids, on the swings. Swinging higher and higher, faster and faster, so you could almost feel, you could jump off and you would fly – but you don't. You hold on tight. We lop off each year backwards and forwards on that swing, and it gets slower and slower and when you finally want to jump – you really want to jump – you're going nowhere, you're stuck.

Pause.

I'm not saying I'm going to fly, but I can't be tied to a bloke who doesn't give a shit and I can't be tied here for the rest of my life.

Wendy   Are you saying you're leaving?

Teresa   No, no – but I have to be free. I have to have a choice when something comes along.

Wendy   What's coming along? What's going to turn up round here?

Scene Four

The flat. **Nick** *and* **Sonny** *sit on the sofa getting stoned.*

Sonny   Good smoke, Nick.

Nick   Lovely.

Sonny   What is it?

Nick   Afghan. I got it from Tony.

Sonny   You took a chance.

Nick   He wouldn't knock me.

Val *enters carrying two bags of shopping.*

Val   Put the kettle on, Sonny.

Sonny   I've just sat down.

Val   You're on that funny stuff again. No wonder you can't get off your arse. Makes your brain go funny. Why everyone slurred their speech in the seventies, years of taking that stuff. Mark my words, Sonny, you'll be a cabbage by the time you're forty.

Sonny *laughs.* **Val** *goes into the kitchen offstage.*

Sonny   I'll be dead then, right, Nicky-boy?

Val *wanders back in.*

Val   Hello there, Nick. I didn't see you when I came in. Do you want some tea?

Nick   Lovely.

Val   Do you want some cake? Don't be shy, there's plenty of it. Sonny'll only stuff it all. It's a victoria sponge.

Nick   Just a small bit.

Val   I'll give you a nice big slice.

She goes out but we can hear her.

How's your mum, Nick?

Nick   She's all right.

Pause. **Val** *begins to hum 'Love Me Do'.*

Sonny   She fucking gets on my tits. Here, take this.

Nick   Cheers. Can you get any more?

Sonny   Reckon I can. Fancy some weed though. Nice bit of skunk.

Nick   Ages since we've had a bit of skunk.

Sonny   Can't beat it. Reckon I might be able to rustle up a couple of deals of whizz an' all. Bobby owes me.

Nick   I can't lug any more of that shit up me nose.

Sonny   Bomb it!

Nick   I'm not taking any more of that shit . . .

Sonny   Stop fucking moaning. It'll do you good. You'll be on your toes and ready to fight the fucking world.

Nick   My prick will shrink up into my stomach.

Sonny   Hark at the stud – Works the other way an' all, you nobber. Get the horn and the old boy'll be up for the week.

Pause. **Val** *enters with a tray. There are three mugs of tea and a sponge cake on the plate.* **Val** *cuts the cake into three and passes the tea and cake round, still humming the song.*

Val   What've you been up to Nick? Still after a job?

Sonny *grins.*

Val   At least he's looking. More than you. You're going to end up in prison – like your dad if he's not careful.

Sonny   I'm going to the top me.

Val   You're going to bloody prison.

Sonny   Piss off.

Val   I've told you. I bet you don't speak to your mother like that, Nick. Not like him – bloody animal.

Sonny   Fuck off.

Val   I've fucking told you!

She tries to stand, but can't — the tray is on her lap. So she throws her cake at **Sonny**, *but it misses.* **Sonny** *throws his cake at* **Val** *and it hits her in the face.* **Sonny** *laughs.* **Val** *wants to laugh, suppresses it, but laughs eventually.*

You sod. Wait till your father comes home.

Sonny   Who, Elvis? — Bollocks!

Pause.

Nick   Have you got a snout?

Sonny   No, last one went in the spliff.

Nick   Shit.

Val   Charlie might have some?

Sonny   No, we just finished his Bensons. I'll get some. Come on, Nick.

Nick   No. I want to stay here. I'm too stoned.

Val   Where are you going?

Sonny   I'm going to get some fags. Do you want anything?

Val   No.

Sonny *gives* **Nick** *the joint and exits. Pause.* **Val** *takes the tray from her lap and moves over to* **Nick** *on the sofa. They kiss tenderly, lovingly.*

Nick   Lovely eyes. Beautiful.

Val *smiles and kisses* **Nick** *passionately. She clambers on top of him and starts to undo his shirt.*

Nick   Leave off a minute, Val.

Nick *moves himself from under her.*

Val   I didn't know you were coming today.

Nick   Sonny'll be back in a minute.

Val   I want you, Nick. Come on, now.

Nick   Leave off.

Val   Give me that.

Val *takes the joint.*

Nick   You don't smoke this.

Val   Yes I do. I need to calm down. You've got me going.

Pause. **Val** *smokes.*

Nick   Give us it back.

Val   I've got an apple pie in the fridge.

Nick   No.

Val   Do you want a slice? Made it for Charlie. Hasn't touched a bit.

Nick   No – really . . .

Val   Are you coming back later on?

Nick   I can't. I've got to sign on.

Pause.

What's that knitting for, Val?

Val   It's for me sister Viv. She's having a baby.

Nick   How old is she?

Val   A bit younger than me – And don't ask.

Nick   I didn't know Sonny had an aunt?

Val   He's got two. Me other sis's called Violet.

Nick   Val, Viv and Violet?

Val   The three Vs. Always used to do 'Bubbles' at the end of the karaoke. See, I'm not such an old biddy.

Nick *smiles.*

Val   Used to go karaoke every week with me sisters. Until Viv met John. Computers, Nick. He works in the city.

Nick   Don't you like him?

Val   No, I like him. It's Charlie who don't like him.

Nick   Bit flash is he?

Val   Well, I think he's all right – But we went to the curry house a couple of years ago when Viv first started going out with him and Charlie didn't take a liking to him. It was awful – I didn't know were to put me eyes. Charlie kept making jokes about the Pakistanis. And he wouldn't drink any wine. Said he might as well write ponce across his head. It weren't too bad till the end. John said he'd treat us but Charlie wouldn't let him. He kept going on about not being bought by a little prick from Highbury. I wouldn't mind but he didn't have any money! And he ripped up John's cheque book!

Nick *grins.*

Val Don't laugh, Nick. That was a week's wages I had to pay. And he had a fight on the bus home. Some Sikh boys broke his arm in two places.

Nick Good old Charlie.

Val Serves him right.

Nick What about the other one?

Val Violet? No – I don't get on with Violet.

Pause.

Nick Can – can I ask you something?

Val You dirty bugger.

Nick No. Something else. I've been thinking.

Val Have you now?

Nick See – I like Charlie.

Val I like Charlie. He's just a lazy bastard.

Nick You know – This, Val.

Val What?

Nick It's out of order – and what about Sonny?

Pause.

I just . . .

Val You want to know? Because you've got a nice bum and I wanted a little comfort.

Nick Charlie's a better man than my dad'll ever be and I'm hardly . . .

Val You've got a cheek. Don't you dare compare yourself to my Charlie. You? You're a boy and you'll never be in the same league as my Charles. I know you, Nick – you're all the same with your grinny look. What do you want me to say? We row, we've got separate beds? No, not good enough. What you want is a fantasy, a real story to toss over . . .

Nick No, Val . . .

Val I know men. I know them too well. I'll tell you what you want. He can't get it up. How do you like that, Nick? Impotent.

Nick I'm sorry, Val.

Val Don't make me laugh.

Pause.

The cleaners all talk about their comforts. What a funny thought – a room full of scrubbers sharing their comforts.

She picks her way round the room clearing up the bits of cake.

I love my tea break. We have such a laugh – fall over laughing. Some of the things Daisy told us this morning about me in the war.

Nick Are you all at it then?

Val Don't say it like that. Makes it sound so sleazy. No. But we all enjoy the stories. Some of them lie sometimes. You can tell – there just isn't that spark in their eyes.

Pause.

What about you, Nick?

Nick What?

Val I mean, you must be able to do better than me? I've heard you're a right little tart.

Nick I don't know . . .

Val Of course you know. It's up there in that little brain of yours.

Nick You're different.

Val I'm old.

Nick You're all right.

Pause.

At home. My mum . . . It's not like here. You and Charlie, friendly and . . . well, Sonny. We're a bit different . . .

Val You can say that again . . .

Nick He's been my best ever mate, Val. Before I met Sonny, I was always the kid who got beaten up at school. I had things straight up here . . . (*Points to his head.*) . . . but I . . . was a fuck-up. My dad. He'd hit me and then he'd buy me stuff, loads of stuff, stuff he couldn't afford . . .

A door slams offstage. Pause. **Sonny** *enters.*

Sonny Oh, Nick!

Nick What?

Sonny Guess who I've just seen down the road. Wendy and Teresa – and guess what, Nicky-boy – they've asked 'us' to meet 'them' for a drink.

Nick Right, great.

Sonny Red Fox. Seven o'clock. Well, for fuck's sake put a smile on your face.

Val He's shy, Sonny. Doesn't want to say much in front of your mum. Not an uncouth sod like you. Don't worry, boys, I'm going into the kitchen.

Val *exits.*

Sonny Let's go down the pub.

Nick I've got to sign on yet.

Sonny So?

Nick   Look, I can't afford it – and anyway, if we go now we'll be well pissed by seven.

Sonny   Don't worry, Nick, I've got fifty knicker.

Nick   Where did you . . .

Sonny   I've sold Tim five Es.

Nick   What?

Sonny   Well, they weren't E, were they. Anadin. Dipped them in some food colour. Told Tim blue Es were new in straight in from Amsterdam. One hundred per cent MDMA.

Nick   He'll do you for that.

Sonny   If he comes anywhere near me I'll cut him – he knows that.

Pause.

Nick   Still, if we go now, we'll be fucked. Wendy and Teresa won't sit there with us rolling around, will they?

Sonny   I don't know . . .

Nick   What if they do? You know Wendy.

Sonny   What?

Nick   She comes on – on heat.

Sonny   On heat?

Nick   You won't be able to get it up, too pissed. She'll laugh at you, Sonny.

Sonny   Don't know about that, Nicky-boy. You know me – ten pints and I could still shaft an elephant.

Pause.

These birds are hot though. Better stick to the spliffs.

Nick   Yeah.

Sonny   Yeah.

Scene Five

*A pub somewhere in east London. Opening music fades into a
continuous juke-box soundtrack.* **Nick** *and* **Sonny** *stand smoking,
and* **Charlie** *enters with three pints.*

Sonny   Cheers, Dad.

Nick   Cheers, Charlie.

Charlie   Get that down, boys. Lovely. So what time are
the ladies turning up?

Sonny   Seven.

Charlie   Fuck. You're bloody keen. It's not half past yet.

Sonny   These birds are quality, Dad.

Charlie   Are they?

Sonny   Not like the other scrubbers round here. Bit of class.

Charlie   Well, boys, let me give you a bit of advice. If
you've not got your hands inside their knickers by closing
time, forget it, class or not.

Sonny   Go on then, Casanova.

Charlie   I tell you, when I was your age the birds knew
where they stood with me – and they respected me for it. But,
then I always was a bit of a smoothie when I was younger.
Should've seen me on my bike. Parker and Fred Perry T-
shirt down at Brighton beach.

Sonny   I thought you was a rocker.

Charlie   Piss off! Rocker! Your mother was the one who
liked Elvis. The king – there was only one king, Pete
Townshend was the king.

Nick   I've seen him on the Woodstock video.

Charlie *breaks into 'My Generation' which* **Sonny** *tries to
interrupt.*

Sonny   Fucking hell, Dad!

Charlie *continues.*

Sonny   Shut up . . .

Charlie *still continues.*

Sonny   If you don't shut up I'm gonna kick your head in!

Charlie *breaks off.*

Charlie   You know, I was told, Roger Daltrey once pissed on my Lambretta.

Sonny   Dad.

Wendy *and* **Teresa** *arrive.* **Charlie** *doesn't notice.*

Charlie   Now, boys, tell me when the girls come in and I'll scarper. But you know, Sonny, I've always had a silver tongue. You could do a lot worse than get me in on the act – their knickers will fall off.

Wendy   Who's the old prick, Sonny?

Charlie   Sonny, you didn't tell me the young ladies had arrived. Hello there, my love.

Wendy *and* **Teresa** *laugh.*

Charlie   Here, look – what did I tell you boys. Now listen, ladies. I was a snake-charmer in a previous life.

Sonny   Fuck off, Dad.

Charlie   It's all under control, boy, leave it to me. Do you like to dance? They used to say I moved like Tom Jones.

Sonny   Oh, shit . . .

Charlie   Now, dear, what's your name?

Wendy   Madonna.

They all laugh except **Sonny***.*

Charlie   Sense of humour! I like a sense of humour in a lady. You know I once knew the Two Ronnies. Painted the town red we did. They autographed a pair of their glasses for me! Shame I can't wear them – right eye seeing the black squiggle, see.

He laughs.

Now, darling, that is a very becoming top you're wearing there. Now what does that say?

He ogles **Wendy**'s *tight top.*

Wendy Never you mind ...

Sonny For fuck's sake!

Charlie Well, ladies ... Listen, I've got to go and have a tinkle – but I'll see you later on.

Sonny Go, Dad, go!

Charlie Ta-ta, girls.

Charlie *exits*.

Teresa Who was that?

Nick Sonny's dad.

Wendy *and* **Teresa** *laugh*.

Sonny No, no – I'll do you, Nick – no because, that bloke ain't my dad. He's my uncle – you know the type – had his last erection when the telly was black and white.

A beat.

So ... Nick, this is Wendy and this is Teresa ...

Wendy
Teresa } All right.

Nick All right.

Wendy I ain't met you before, have I?

Nick No, I've seen you about.

Wendy Yeah.

Sonny Yeah. So what have you been up to then?

Teresa Not much.

Sonny Yeah?

Wendy Not much – we went down Edgware Road.

Sonny Oh right. Yeah, sounds great. Me and Nick have been at work. You were lucky you caught me at the corner. I was just on my way back to the site.

Nick How comes you weren't at work?

Wendy I get Friday afternoon off of the salon.

Teresa I heard you and Nick got laid off?

Sonny No, no – who told you that? That was ages ago. This is a different firm – and it's more dosh.

Wendy Yeah?

Nick Oh yeah, that's right . . .

Sonny No darkies either.

Pause.

Would you two like a drink while I go to the bar?

Teresa No, we can't stop long.

Wendy Yes we will. I'll have a double Tia Maria and Coke and Teresa'll have a double vodka and lime . . .

Nick Doubles!

Sonny D'you want crisps? I know you like prawn cocktail, Wend.

Teresa No.

Sonny Give us a hand with the drinks, Nick.

Sonny *and* **Nick** *exit. Pause.*

Teresa Fucking hell, Wendy . . .

Wendy They're all right.

Teresa Jesus, they're like Pinky and Perky.

Wendy We're not going. I want to talk to Nick.

Pause.

I know you used to fancy Sonny, whatever you say.

Teresa That was before I had a brain. I thought Simon Bates was sexy and I still listened to Bros.

Wendy *laughs*.

Teresa I preferred it when the old boy was here. At least I was having a laugh.

Wendy We'll have the drink and we can say you're feeling sick. I can't stay that late anyway, I'm up at six for Bognor tomorrow.

Teresa Listen. I'm not saying I'm sick. I'm fed up with getting you out of shit. You can explain to them.

Wendy Getting me out of shit? I don't want to go.

Pause.

Have you come on yet?

Teresa *shakes her head.*

Wendy What you going to do?

Teresa I don't know.

Wendy Get rid of it . . .

Teresa Don't say it like that. It's a baby.

Wendy No it's not. It's just a load of . . .

Teresa What?

Wendy I don't know. But it's not a baby.

Pause.

I can't wait to get away from that pissing salon.

Teresa I don't know how you put up with it.

Wendy And I always wanted to be a hairdresser.

Teresa You're not serious?

Wendy After air stewardess, Trese, then nurse – oh, and a nun. Course I'm not serious! Dandruff, scabby, leering old men and the blue-rinse brigade are not my idea of fun.

Teresa Get out then.

Wendy I need the money.

Teresa We all need the money.

Pause.

Wendy   I wanted to be a secretary.

Teresa *laughs.*

Wendy   I would've an' all if college hadn't chucked me out.

Teresa   You can't even spell let alone type.

Wendy   What I need is to meet someone very rich to take me to Hollywood. Nice big stretch limo, house in Beverly Hills, and a fucking great tit job. Oh yes, I could do with meeting a bloke who could give me that . . .

Sonny *and* **Nick** *enter with the drinks.*

Sonny   They didn't have any prawn cocktail, Wend.

Nick   There you go.

Wendy   Cheers.

Teresa   Cheers.

Teresa *downs her drink.*

Sonny   Do you always swallow that fast?

Teresa   Are you trying to be funny?

Sonny   Don't get your knickers in a twist, Trese.

Teresa   Have you always been running on just the two brain cells or are you down to the one?

Wendy   Trese!

Sonny   Just joking – a joke, Trese!

Pause.

Guess what girls – If you fancy it – We can go back to Nick's flat.

Nick   Sonny . . .

Sonny   No one'll be in – and I've got a bottle of Jack Daniel's in Nick's motor.

Wendy   Sounds great.

Teresa   You're leaving early tomorrow, Wend.

Wendy   No, not that early.

Sonny   Never know, Trese, if you're game for a laugh, Nick might let you swallow it all in one.

Teresa   What did you say?

Sonny   Just having a giggle.

Teresa   Fuck off, Sonny. You just can fuck off! Come on, Wend . . .

Sonny   Do what?

Teresa   Drink up, we're going.

Wendy   Trese . . .

Sonny   We just . . .

Nick   It's all right, Sonny . . .

Wendy   Wait a minute . . .

Teresa   I'm going.

Sonny   You can't go.

Teresa   Well, we are. I could have a better time with a couple of stiffs down Manor Park cemetery.

Sonny   You've only been here five minutes.

Wendy   Teresa . . .

Teresa   Come on, Wend!

Nick   Go on, piss off!

Wendy *and* **Teresa** *exit.*

Sonny   Nick, you prat! They can't do that.

Shouting after them.

You fucking slags, come back here!

Pause.

Well, fuck off then! Go on, piss off you old-doers!

Nick   Shut up, Sonny, we'll be barred.

Sonny   You wait. When I see that Teresa I'm going to give her a slap. Fucking bitch.

Pause. **Charlie** *enters.*

Charlie   All right there. Hello? Where's the totty gone? I've been gone five minutes and they've left – What did you say to them?

Sonny   Nothing.

Charlie   Nothing? Well, it's a crying shame, boy – I didn't half fancy a Donald.

Pause.

Sonny   Anyway, they're dykes.

Charlie   Never!

Sonny   Everyone knows – 'strap it on' merchants.

Charlie   Well, you never can tell. I knew a dyke once. Lovely she was – what I would've done to give her one. Still, a man can't have every woman.

Sonny   Course you can. If you got the spondooli anything's possible. Thirty quid and your train fare to King's Cross – you've got a low-life with a dose. Thirty million and a yacht and Fergie will be sucking your cock.

Charlie *thinks about it.*

Charlie   I don't like Fergie. She's ginger. There are some things you can't buy, boys. A dyke's a dyke. But, look at me and your mother, Sonny. Now you can't buy that twenty-five years' worth.

Sonny   Shut up, Dad. You were probably the reason why they left early.

Nick   Don't worry, Sonny.

Sonny   You sill old tosser . . .

Charlie   Sonny . . .

Nick   Like you never said a fucking word, Sonny . . .

Pause.

Come on – you've still got the nifty.

A beat.

Let's get really pissed.

Sonny   Yeah . . . Yeah, let's get really pissed.

Scene Six

Nick *and* **Sonny** *wait for a bus on the street. They are very drunk.*

Sonny   Nicky-boy.

Nick   Sonny-boy.

Sonny   How long's the bus? I'm going to puke.

Nick   No, no – you don't want to do that.

Sonny   Deep breaths.

He takes in gulps of air.

That's better.

Nick   Does it work?

Sonny   Yeah.

Nick *takes in gulps of air.*

Nick   I feel sick.

Sonny   No, no. You're not doing it right. Like this –

He shows him and **Nick** *copies.*

That's it. That's it.

Nick   This country's shit, Sonny. Look at it. Fucking shit everywhere. All over the floor. They can't even empty the bins. All the shit blowing around.

Sonny   No. That was me. You've got to do the bins on the way home. Wouldn't be a night out without doing the bins – and the aerials – we'll do the aerials an' all. Tell you what, Nicky-boy, if you do a Porsche I'll give you a hundred quid.

Nick   Yeah?

Sonny   Yeah. I will an' all.

Nick   This country is shit.

Sonny   No. No it's not. Greatest country in the world, England. We won the war, didn't we? And the fucking Argies. And them fucking Arab-cunts.

He starts to sing 'Rule Britannia' drunkenly.

Ben, *a young bloke a bit older than* **Sonny** *and* **Nick**, *enters eating some chips.*

Sonny   Oi, oi. All right mate! We've been singing, haven't we, Nicky-boy – 'Rule Britannia'. Had a night out, have you? We have. We're pissed.

Ben   Yeah, mate, nice.

Sonny   Yeah, nice.

Ben   All right there, mate? Look like you're going to fall over –

Sonny (*laughing*)   Not me, cocker . . .

Pause.

Oi, mate – you got a fag?

Ben   No, mate.

Sonny   Go on – give us a fag.

Ben   No, mate – I don't smoke.

Sonny   Oi, Nicky-boy. He don't smoke . . .

A beat.

Oi, mate, give us a chip.

Ben (*laughing – to* **Nick**)   Oi is your mate taking the piss?

Pause.

Sonny   Am I black or what? Oi, give us a chip.

Ben   Leave off, mate . . .

Nick   Sonny . . .

Sonny   Give us a chip . . .

Ben   Leave it out, mate . . .

Sonny   Give us a fucking chip . . .

Ben   Piss off . . .

Sonny   You tight cunt . . .

Sonny *tries to grab some.*

Ben   Piss off you wanker . . .

Sonny   You fucking tight cunt . . .

Nick   No, Sunny . . .

Ben   Oh yeah . . .

Sonny   You cunt . . .

Ben (*pulling a knife*)   Fuck off before I cut you.

He throws the chips and frees his other hand.

I mean it, you prick!

Nick   Sonny . . .

Sonny   Silly boy . . . Silly boy . . .

Sonny *and* **Ben** *square up to each other at a safe distance, then the stand-off begins. Each moves waiting to pick his moment.* **Sonny** *lunges at* **Ben** *and catches him off balance. They struggle and fall to the ground.* **Sonny** *gets the upper hand.* **Ben** *drops the knife which* **Sonny** *takes hold of as he takes control. The lights begin to fade.*

Silly boy . . . Silly boy . . . I'm going to cut you up, you cunt.

Ben   No . . . No . . . No . . . No . . . !

Blackout. **Ben** *screams.*

Scene Seven

Police sirens wail and flashing blue lights bathe the stage. **Charlie** *stands alone and eats a kebab. He is very drunk.*

Charlie   Oi, Copper! Copper! I hope you're going to catch the bastard who did that! Hey – copper! Copper! (*Pause.*) Cunt . . . Fucking shit . . . (*Pause.*) Law . . . Not my fucking

law, you bastards! (*Pause.*) You want my dole . . . Have it . . .
Fucking have it, you bastards . . .

*He unsteadily reaches with his free hand into a pocket and then tosses
out his change and a crumpled-up note.*

Have it . . . (*Pause.*) I'd rather have the shit off your shoes,
copper . . . You wait . . . There will be the day when I hold the
keys to your fucking cell, copper! And, copper – you won't
get any grub either! (*Pause.*) I remember you . . . I seen you at
the dogs with your missis . . . you ain't so proud then . . .

Pause. He reflects drunkenly.

Poor kid . . . Could've been my Sonny. (*Pause.*) Blood on the
streets . . . That's what they said . . . (*Pause.*) Blood like shit on
my hands, copper . . . (*Throws his kebab.*)

Look at 'em . . . Wank, wank, wank, wank, wank . . . Val . . .
Val . . . Fuck her . . .

He laughs loudly at himself.

Can't even manage a fucking toss . . . Charlie Jaffa, right,
copper . . . Charlie Jaffa, but I dances like Tom Jones . . .

*He stumbles around stupidly, but then starts to spin, faster and faster,
till he falls. Pause. He doesn't move and he moans with pain.*

Help, copper, help . . . I hurt me leg.

He cries with terrible, searing pain – from the gut.

Fucked it now . . . Fuck, fuck, fuck . . . (*Pause.*) God! Someone
listen to me! Just a hand . . . I hurt!

*He is drowned out by a wailing siren which at first offers hope, but
gradually fades into nothing.*

Act Two

Scene One

Nick *and* **Val** *sit on the park bench.*

Val Just fancied some fresh air. You know.

Nick Yeah.

Val On my way to see Charlie.

Nick Is he all right? Sonny said it was a broken ankle.

Val Fracture.

A beat.

He can be a miserable bastard when he's ill.

Nick How long is he in for?

Val Just a couple of days. It's a nasty break.

Nick I'll get him a card.

Val Don't you bloody dare! It serves the bugger right! He won't be going to the pub for a while, I can tell you that for sure.

Nick Is he all right?

Val He's bloody loving it, Nick. And don't ask me why – but the nurses are like flies round shit. I went in to see him yesterday morning and the soppy sod was singing 'Love Me Tender' to a little group of them. He followed it with his two favourite Ronnie Barker jokes, and the dirty sod asked them if they wanted to draw straws for the first bed bath! And he didn't notice me standing there. I don't know what's wrong with them. They've all signed his plaster.

Pause.

Are you coming over tomorrow?

Nick I don't know, Val.

Val   Right.

Nick   I mean, I don't know what I'm doing yet. I'll try to get over.

Pause.

Val   Is it someone else?

Nick   What?

Val   Have you met someone? Look, you don't have to lie . . .

Nick   I haven't.

Val   Hark at me. Stupid, jealous old woman.

Nick   No, Val.

Pause.

Val   You're my greatest pleasure and my greatest curse. Do you know that, Nick?

Nick   I don't understand.

Val   Being with you. It sends a shiver of excitement up my back, you make me laugh, you listen to me, you make me feel . . . I don't have any words for how you make me feel, Nick, but when I look in the mirror doing me hair I think about you and I smile.

Pause.

I see the wrinkles and I think of you . . .

Pause.

I'm old, Nick. I have grey hairs in my head, and the vanity of believing that you could love me, the things I think of. Leaving Charlie, Jesus, Charlie, he couldn't survive . . . I don't know where I am or where I'm going, Nick, but every time I'm with you, I can't help thinking – How many times will I see you again and is this the last time and it's driving me mad, Nick, because as the evenings draw in, and the days go by I think, is this the last time I'll be with a man, and is this the last time I'll love someone. It doesn't matter to me whether you care a jot for me, but the day I stop loving, the day I stop caring . . . The day I don't want to care . . . That frightens me, Nick. Because I will have become one of them.

Nick Who, Val?

Val Out there. Like the rest that go on and on and on, day after day . . . I used to think . . . I mean, I thought that my men, my boys, were the sparkle. The thing that put the twinkle in my eye.

Pause.

But this morning when I was going through cupboards looking for a puzzle for Charlie, I found something. Ages, years ago I had a boyfriend who worked in London Zoo, I didn't see him for long, but he was such a laugh, such fun. We even screwed in the giraffe enclosure one night. He bought me a present, a tiger bear, and I kept it.

Pause.

When I saw that bear this morning, it made me cry. The memories, things I hadn't thought of for years . . . I felt the way you make me feel.

Pause.

I realised then, that what I have been doing, year after year is fooling myself – kidding myself. With every bloke there comes new promise, and I do work at it, I give them everything I have here. And they . . . They come and go. They go, Nick. Just like you will . . .

Nick I won't, Val . . .

Val But I still dream, I still . . . Christ. It's so stupid, so stupid. You're twenty, for God's sake and you haven't been the first young one either.

Long pause.

Nick What's in the brown bag, Val?

Val Just some cake.

Nick Oh.

Val   Made it for Charlie. Put bloody cream and chocolate on it as well. Still didn't eat it. Had his fall, didn't he? It's gone stale, Nick.

Pause.

I'm going to feed it to the birds.

Nick   I used to feed the birds when I was a kid with me mum. Remember, they used to have lovely great swans then, Val.

Val   All gone now.

Nick   Like the bandstand. Used to play soldiers in the bandstand.

Val   Still got the playground.

Nick   Kids still play, Val.

Val   Mums still watch them.

Pause.

Did anything happen on Friday night, Nick?

Nick   No, Val.

Val   It's just Sonny's jeans ...

Nick   No – nothing.

Val   And what with Charlie ...

Nick   Nothing happened.

Pause.

Val   Did you know it's my birthday tomorrow, Nick?

Nick   No, Sonny hasn't said.

Val   Suppose it's why I'm being so ... I haven't enjoyed a birthday in years.

Nick   I'll come over ...

Val   You don't have to.

Nick   It'll be great. We'll have a laugh. I've got some money left from me giro. I'll get a bottle of plonk. Anyway, reckon I might be able to get some work. Council are taking on at the tip.

Val   I've got to go. Charlie will wonder where I am.

She stands.

Tomorrow then.

Nick   Yeah.

Val *bends down to kiss his cheek, but* **Nick** *directs his mouth towards hers. Pause.* **Val** *exits.*

Scene Two

Nick *and* **Sonny** *sit on the park bench.*

Sonny   I've been thinking, Nicky-boy.

Nick   When did that happen then?

Sonny   No. I'm serious. They should make me Prime Minister.

Nick   You!

Sonny   Yeah, I'd be great.

Nick   You'd make Hitler look like the Tooth Fairy.

Sonny   I'd be the bollocks. You wait and see. Be brilliant. Holidays in Spain for everyone except the posh people – they're going to Blackpool. Legalise hash, 'n big newspapers and satellite telly in every house. If you don't have a dish you get your nuts chopped off and if you're a bird you lose one tit.

Nick *laughs.*

Sonny   Excellent. Imagine everyone in the country all able to watch the cricket series. I'll tell you one thing, Nicky-boy, the darkies can't half play cricket. Viv Richards – what a player he was! Black as the ace of spades though.

Nick   Why do you hate the blacks so much?

Sonny   Just do. Always have. Hate the Pakis more though.

Nick No – Why?

Sonny What do you mean, why? Hark at Ken Livingstone!

Nick No, but why?

Sonny What? Piss off, Nick. Don't give me that lefty shit . . .

Nick What shit?

Sonny The only reason they're any good at cricket is because they've got more monkey in them than us – Makes them bowl faster.

Nick I'm not a fucking lefty.

Sonny You sound like it.

Nick So what are you, Sonny?

Pause.

Sonny Stoned.

Nick Don't fuck about.

Sonny I'm not talking about this.

Nick Why?

Sonny Politics is crap.

Nick No, Sonny. What are you? Who the fuck are you, Sonny?

Sonny You know what I'd do? I'd sling all the darkies and Pakis out, the Kurds can go, and the fucking Greeks. There are enough of them around.

Nick So?

Sonny There must be millions of blacks here now, Nicky-boy. We should have England just like it used to be. This country's going down the swanny. We should be the best – For fuck's sake, we didn't even qualify for the World Cup!

Nick It'll never change, Sonny.

Sonny Yes it will. You know it will, Nick, just a matter of time. Just think, Nicky-boy. The more foreigners I do, the more I scare, the more they're off back to jumba-jumba land. It's simple. The loony-lefties down the council are just interested in looking after the coons. My dad's told me about Enoch Powell. He'd've slung them all out.

Nick It's not that easy, Sonny.

Sonny Yes it is. If they are going to stay here we should give them a couple of sheets of corrugated iron and a packet of nails and let them build their shanty towns down the road.

Nick But, Sonny . . .

Sonny They'll be all right. What happens if you lose a dog. It doesn't suddenly die, does it? It survives and gets a bit here and there. The foreigners will do the same. They live like animals anyway. People can look after themselves. White people do it as well. I'm all right, I've never worked proper – and I don't want to either. Charlie's been in and out of work all his life, we're sweet. Come on, Nick – I can go on to the estate get two ounces of resin on tick and by five o'clock I've earnt a ton and got a deal for myself. Dad gets a few quid on the side down at the dogs. Don't need a job. Got the dole. I can live. If I knock someone every now and again, then who gives a shit. You've got to look after number one, mate.

Pause.

Nick Sonny.

Sonny Yeah.

Pause.

Well, spit it out.

Nick I . . .

Sonny What?

Nick I need a change.

Sonny What do you mean?

Nick What do we do?

Sonny   Don't know.

Nick   Sit about.

Sonny   Not all the time.

Nick   Get stoned.

Sonny   It's all right. We have a grin.

Nick   Yeah.

Pause.

Last Friday. The bloke at the bus stop.

Sonny   That prick with the chips?

Sonny *laughs*.

Nick   Yeah.

Sonny   What about him?

Nick   You didn't have to cut him, Sonny.

Sonny   Yes I did. I always cut them.

Nick   No.

Sonny   What the fuck's the matter with you?

Nick   It just pisses me off, that's all.

Sonny   Don't get moody on me, Nick. He was an arsehole. He pulled the blade on me. He deserved it.

Nick   He was all right.

Sonny   No way.

Nick   It weren't about that . . . That, that was about enjoying it, seeing the blood.

Sonny   Don't give me this shit.

Nick   He was screaming like a baby, Sonny, like a baby. All that blood pissing out of his mouth. You enjoyed it.

Sonny   No.

Nick   Yes you did, you loved it, you always do. You always do. That . . . That was . . .

Sonny   Fuck you, Nick!

Nick   That was shit, Sonny, that was shit! And we always do it. We always do it, Sonny! I do it, you do it – it's bad, Sonny, it's bad.

Sonny   Yeah, we do it. We do it, Nick. So fucking what? You should think about where you stand. Who your mates are.

Pause.

Nick   Yeah. Like I said, I'm pissed off.

Long pause.

They want someone down the tip to do a bit of refuse collection. I'm thinking of going after it.

Sonny   You don't want that . . .

Nick   Get some work, have a bit of money.

Sonny   You're all right.

Nick   I want to do some normal stuff for a while.

Pause.

Sonny   It's down to you.

A beat.

You're a mug if you do though.

Nick   I ain't had me car a week, Sonny. I don't want to sell it, but I can't afford it.

Sonny   You've got things sorted as it is. Bits of pocket money. Live at home, what d'you want to spend your life clearing up shit for?

Nick   I don't know.

Pause.

Sonny   You . . . You're my mate, Nick.

Nick   I know, Sonny.

Pause.

Sonny　Let's go down the pub.

Nick　No, Sonny.

Sonny　Look, if you're a bit hard up, I know a geezer who's got five hundred trips he wants to knock out. I mean that stuff got your car in the first place. You know the new under-eighteen night in Ilford? – Well, I've heard they're crying out for some acid down there.

Nick　Yeah?

Sonny　Yeah. Little kids having their experiments – you'll make a bomb. The only reason I haven't been down there is because they won't let me in.

Nick　You're twenty as it is.

Sonny　It's because of my barnet. Get down there. Gap in the market, Nicky-boy. Use your noddle, mate, make your own luck. Stay on the trips for a couple of months. If it's all going all right start taking a few Es with you. That Escort will be a Porsche by the time you're twenty-one. Gap in the market – serve it up and knock it out, Nicky-boy. Sweet as a nut.

Nick *looks at his feet.*

Sonny　You're my mate, Nick.

Scene Three

Sonny *sits on the sofa in the flat reading the* Sun. *Pause. A door slams offstage and* **Val** *enters with* **Ryan**. *He's a few years older than* **Sonny** *and carries some of* **Val**'s *shopping.*

Val　Look who I bumped into, Sonny.

Sonny *turns.*

Sonny　Jesus! All right, Ryan, mate.

Val　I saw him coming out of Tesco's. And I said to him – you must come back for some tea and a slice of cake.

She takes the bags from **Ryan**.

Tea, Ryan? Sonny?

Ryan   Yes please, Val.

Val *exits.*

Sonny   Jesus – Look at you . . .

Ryan   You all right, Sonny?

Sonny   Yeah – I can't believe it. You haven't changed.

Ryan   Neither have you.

Pause. He sits down on the sofa.

So are you working?

Sonny   No – Did a bit on the side a couple of months ago. But that's it. Nothing for ages. What you up to?

Ryan   Not much. Bit of voluntary work for Mencap.

Sonny   Bloody hell! All right, Mother Teresa?

Ryan *smiles.*

Sonny   Still down there are you?

Ryan   Where?

Sonny   Uni-ver-sity. That's where you went, weren't it.

Ryan   No, I finished a couple of years ago. But I decided to stay on and live there, like . . .

Sonny   Wolverhampton? That's a bit of a shit-hole, ain't it?

Ryan *laughs.* **Sonny** *grins.*

Sonny   Mind you, you always had a nut and bolt missing.

Ryan   Yeah?

Sonny   Well, I mean if it's a trial for Middlesex, or . . . What did you do?

Ryan   Sociology and economics . . .

Sonny   Or that at fucking Wolverhampton, what would you do?

Ryan   I'd do the same again, Sonny . . .

Sonny   Well, I mean doing a bit for a few dribblers ain't all that, is it?

Pause.

Mad you was, Ryan. I would have given my right bollock for a trial at Middlesex . . .

Ryan   I know.

Sonny   Yeah . . .

Ryan   I wanted to get away from London, Sonny.

Pause.

Sonny   Five years is a long time, mate.

Pause.

Ryan   I went over the park earlier.

Sonny   Yeah?

Ryan   When I think of all the time I spent over there with you lot I can't believe it . . .

Sonny   Who ever heard of a cricket team from Hackney – What my dad always said.

Pause.

Ryan   How is Charlie?

Sonny   You know Charlie, West Ham, the dog track and a bottle of cheap Scotch. That's my old man. Soppy sod's gone and fractured his ankle . . .

Ryan   I wondered if I'd see him over there . . .

Sonny   The dogs? No – he ain't over there much now.

Ryan   I had a wander round all the old places this morning. They were running some trials, Sonny. I saw the porter sweeping up in the stand still the same. The old sod used to give me fifty pee for a bet when I was a kid.

Pause.

Saw a weird thing. They was getting ready for the first heat
and I was buzzing – well, I ain't been the dogs since I left.
The hare, right, it shot up the track, but as it turned the
corner it slowed and slowed, Sonny. Something must've been
wrong with the power. But the dogs – they caught up – and
they caught it. They ripped it apart, Sonny.

Pause.

Sonny   Well, it weren't a real rabbit, was it? You want to
see a greyhound get hold of a cat . . .

Ryan   It stuck right in my head. I was thinking about it
when I went over the park. I sat down on a bench next to the
playground and had a fag. I was thinking over the cricket an'
that – the kids team, you know, Sonny?

Sonny   We wasn't kids . . .

Ryan   I used to dream that one day I'd be Ian Botham or
Viv Richards. But your dad's right, Sonny. Kids round here
don't play cricket. They shovel shit.

Pause.

Something else I noticed – and it took me ages to work it out
cos I knew I was in a funny mood and I didn't know if it was
me. But it weren't. It was the playground, Sonny – a
playground. No children in it.

Val *enters with a tray with three mugs of tea and cake cut in three bits.*

Val   You could've done the washing up, Sonny.

Sonny *and* **Ryan** *take a mug and a piece of cake each.* **Val** *sits down
with the tray.*

Ryan   Cheers, Val.

Val   I thought you'd come back all posh, Ryan . . .

Ryan   You've only got to be back here a day and the accent
comes right back.

Val   Still playing cricket, are you, Ryan?

Ryan   Just an odd Sunday morning . . .

Val   I used to enjoy our chats, Ryan. I missed your company when you left – and I was worried, wasn't I Sonny? You did so well in your O levels . . .

Ryan   A levels Val . . .

Val   And we didn't see you any more.

Pause.

You used to bring Sonny home from cricket practice and I'd make you sausage and chips.

Ryan   That's right – rice pudding for afters . . .

Sonny   Flake on top an' all . . .

Ryan   I don't eat sausages any more.

Val   Neither do I. All the mad cow stuff . . .

Ryan   Good old British beef – rotten to the core. It's me other half actually. She's a vegetarian.

Sonny   You're knocking off a veggie!

Val   Shut up, Sonny. You've got a girlfriend, Ryan?

Ryan   It's a bit more than that now. We're getting married.

Pause.

Why I came back. You know, doing the rounds . . .

Sonny   You should've brought her over, Ry, I bet she's a right stunner, eh, Mum? Ryan always got the birds . . .

Ryan *grins.*

Sonny   What's her name then?

Ryan   Sharman.

Sonny   Sharman? That's a funny name. Sounds like a bloody wog.

Ryan *looks at his feet embarrassed.*

Sonny   Get on – you've not shacked up with a fucking jungle bunny?

Val   Will you shut up your foul mouth!

Long pause.

Ryan   Still have a knockabout with a bat, Sonny?

Sonny   No.

Ryan   Right.

Sonny   Don't play no more. Still like to watch it on the telly though . . .

Ryan   Yeah?

Sonny   Hang about with Nick now.

Ryan   He wasn't in the cricket team?

Sonny   No – you know him though. His dad had the chippie in Mare Street.

Ryan   That bloke. He was a crazy!

Sonny   Still is. Knocks his missis about, and Nick.

Val   I don't know how she puts up with it. She was black and blue when I saw her in Dalston last week.

Sonny   I've said to Nick, if he wants me to have a word, a few of the lads'll go and pay a visit.

Val   I've told you, Sonny . . .

Sonny   He'll piss himself.

Val   She should go to the social.

Sonny   You can't go beating up women. You've got to have a few principles.

Ryan   You haven't changed, Sonny.

Sonny   I mean, if he wants to crack a few soots' heads together . . .

Pause.

Ryan   So what's this Nick like then?

Val   He's a lovely boy. Sonny's best mate. And he's not sitting about on his arse like Sonny. He wants to get out and about and do things – like you, Ryan . . .

Sonny   Yeah. He's got some brains – and he's a good laugh, like.

Val   He's a bit like you, Ryan.

Sonny   Most of the time he's there and right bang on for you but sometimes it's like coming up against a brick wall. You just can't talk to him.

Ryan   S'pose it's the old man?

Sonny   Yeah.

Pause.

Ryan   Have you still got the David Gower gloves?

Sonny   I wouldn't part with them for the world.

Ryan   I had to queue two hours to get them signed for you.

Sonny   They're in me room. Shall I get them?

Ryan   Yeah.

Val   They're not there any more.

Sonny   What?

Val   They're not there.

Sonny   Where are they?

Val   Your dad took them down the car boot sale a couple of years ago.

Sonny   No –

Val   You said he could take them. He got a fiver –

Sonny   That's all the cricket stuff I had left. Oh no! I wouldn't have let him sell them. They were my David Gower gloves. I wouldn't . . .

Val   Yes you did. I remember – there were some records, the gloves, some Lego bricks and a Darth Vader . . .

Sonny   I don't believe it.

Pause.

I loved those gloves. They were the best thing I ever had.
You remember?

Ryan   Yeah.

Sonny   Always scored sixes with my David Gowers.

Pause.

You're fucking lying!

Val   Sonny!

Ryan   Sonny . . .

Sonny's *up on his feet and facing* **Val**.

Sonny   You fucking bitch! You fucking lying bitch!

He grabs **Val**'s *mug which he throws down on to the floor and smashes.*

You always do this to me! Take my things! You didn't ask
me, you didn't!

Val   Sonny, I promise you . . .

Ryan   Come on, Sonny – They were just gloves.

Sonny   They were my David Gowers.

Ryan   Come on, Sonny. Leave it . . .

Sonny   Oh piss off!

Sonny *turns and exits fast.* **Ryan** *goes to follow, but stops. Pause.*

Val   I'm sorry about Sonny.

Ryan *nods.*

Ryan   I should go.

Val *nods. Pause.*

Ryan   I'll be off then.

Val   I missed you, Ryan. You could've got in touch . . .

Ryan   I couldn't. Charlie . . .

Val   When are you going home?

Ryan   Next week.

Val   You can come over in the week if you like? I'll bake something. Give us a ring and I'll stick the kettle on . . .

Ryan   No, Val.

Pause.

See you then, Val.

Ryan *turns and exits.* **Val** *stands and puts the tray on the floor. She gets on her knees and scoops some of the broken crockery with her hand. She looks at a piece.*

Val   Shit.

She discards the piece and reaches for her slice of half-eaten cake.

Scene Four

Wendy *and* **Teresa** *sit on the park bench.*

Wendy   Look, don't tell Freddie – You don't know yet, Trese . . .

Teresa   Well, if I'm not pregnant it won't matter anyway – will it?

Pause.

I'm not getting rid of it, Wend.

Wendy   But if you tell Freddie he might want you to get rid of it . . .

Teresa   Well, then he can fuck off!

Pause.

Wendy   I don't think that bloke I met in Bognor was up to much, eh, Trese? He's a bouncer for a club in Peckham, Trese . . .

Teresa   I know. You told me already.

Pause.

Wendy   Bloody bastard tried to stick his hands in me knickers soon as I grabbed hold of him. I said to him – you fucking dare and I'll have your bollocks, mate . . .

Teresa (*smiling*)   You never told me that?

Wendy   Well . . . You were death-warmed-up all weekend and I've never heard anyone moan like it . . .

Teresa   Don't rub it in.

Sonny *enters. He has a cheap bunch of flowers. He pauses as he notices* **Teresa**.

Sonny   All right.

Wendy   She's going in a minute . . .

Teresa   You didn't tell me you were meeting Sonny . . .

Sonny   Yeah – well. We're going to the pub, like.

Pause.

Well, go on then – Piss off, Trese . . .

Wendy   Sonny!

Teresa   It's all right. I'll leave you to it, Wendy – I know when I'm not wanted . . .

She gets up.

Better offer than boring – Wend . . .

Wendy   No . . .

Teresa   I don't need it.

Teresa *exits.*

Wendy   Teresa!

Pause. **Sonny** *wanders over to the park bench and sits down. Pause.*

Sonny   Cheers for coming, Wend.

Wendy   Don't call me Wend. My name's Wendy.

Sonny   Wendy – I'm sorry.

Wendy   What do you want?

Sonny   The pub – I'm sorry. The bloke who turned up.

Wendy   Who, your uncle?

Sonny   Yeah. Well, no. He's not my uncle. He's my dad.

Wendy   So?

Sonny   Well, I know he embarrassed you and Trese.

Wendy   Oh yeah?

Sonny   We were all right till he turned up.

Wendy   Was that it?

Sonny   What, Wend? I'm trying to say sorry.

Wendy   I don't care if he's your dad.

Sonny   I brought you some flowers.

Pause.

Wendy   Who told you to do that?

Sonny   I thought of them.

Wendy   Great imagination.

Sonny   Don't take the piss. I thought you would like them.

Wendy   Like I said, great imagination.

Sonny   Why did you come here if you just want to take the piss?

Wendy   Because I'm as fucking sad as you are.

Pause.

Sonny   You met me at the pub.

Wendy   My whole life revolves around washing hair for one-fifty an hour. For a minute the thought of going out for a drink sounded exciting.

Pause.

Sonny   You went Bognor, didn't you?

Wendy   Fucking shit that was. Pissed down all day
Saturday and all day Sunday and Teresa didn't stop
moaning.

Sonny   I don't know why you hang about with her,
Wend...

Wendy   Silly bitch thinks she's pregnant.

Sonny   Teresa? I thought she was right frigid.

Wendy   Yeah – well... She just pisses me off sometimes,
that's all...

Pause.

Sonny   Me Aunt Viv had her baby yesterday. They're
calling it Alexandria.

Wendy   Alexandria?

Sonny   Shit, innit?

Pause.

I reckon that – that you would feel better about things if you
had someone.

Wendy   What?

Sonny   A bloke, like.

Wendy *laughs.*

Sonny   I can't say this very good. But – I think you're –
beautiful.

Wendy   Shit. You just don't give up.

Sonny   I well fancy you, Wend...

Wendy *laughs.*

Sonny   Don't fucking laugh at me! I mean it!

Pause.

Wendy   You're unreal.

Sonny   I mean it, Wend. I've always liked you.

Wendy   No, Sonny.

Sonny Come on, Wend, give us a go.

Wendy I'm not a piece of meat, Sonny.

Sonny I really mean it, Wendy.

Pause.

I've got some dough on me now. We could go up west, go to the pictures in Leicester Square, it'll be great.

Wendy If I wanted to be bought I'd be knocking about down Commerical Road.

Sonny I would pay anything in the world to have you.

Pause. **Sonny** *takes out a packet of cigarettes, gives one to* **Wendy**, *puts one in his own mouth and then takes out a box of matches. He shakes it. No sound — it's empty.*

You got a match, Wend?

Wendy My arse, your face.

Sonny *grins and* **Wendy** *lights the cigarette with her Zippo.*

Sonny Look at the kids over there, Wend. I used to be like that. Used to stand on top of the slide, look all around me at London. All them flats.

Pause. **Sonny** *pulls out his hanky and blows his nose making a disgusting noise.*

Wendy Sonny, that's disgusting. You're just like my brother.

Sonny Jimmy? Thought you'd disowned him.

Wendy No.

Sonny He's a fucking disgrace.

Wendy You've got a cheek. He's not gay. He's just confused.

Sonny That's what they all say. Just you keep him away from the school gates . . .

Wendy Piss off!

Pause.

Sonny   I didn't want to upset you, Wend – just a joke.

Wendy   No more jokes, Sonny.

Pause.

If anyone's queer you are. Stuck to Nick like glue you are.
Like his arse, do you? Don't blame you. He's got a great arse.

Sonny   What?

Wendy   Got a great arse Nick.

Sonny   You fancy him . . .

Wendy   So?

Sonny   You're after Nick. The cunt, he knows I . . .

Wendy   What?

Sonny   Bastard, all that shit about the bird at the chip shop
and it was you.

Wendy   So what are you trying to say, Sonny?

Sonny   Cunt, I'll have him for this.

Wendy   You lay a finger on Nick.

Pause.

Sonny   Good in the sack, was he? Got a big prick, has he?

Wendy   Leave off, Sonny.

Sonny   Come on, Wend, don't get all shy on me. You've
never been one to hold it all in before, I've heard your filth in
the pub.

Wendy   I really want to fuck Nick. I wank over him in the
bath. I want to suck him off and I want him to fuck me till I
cry. Are you satisfied now, Sonny!

Pause.

Don't try and look upset, Sonny, you don't give a shit about
Nick. I know you too well.

Pause.

It's been up there in your little brain for at least a year, hasn't it, Sonny?

Sonny   Leave it alone now, Wend –

Wendy   No, Sonny, I've never liked you. You think everyone's against you, betraying you, using you, Sonny, just like you think Nick is. But you use people – and when you've had enough of them you just smash them in. I know you, Sonny.

Sonny   No – you don't know me. No one knows me!

Pause.

I came here to say what I meant. Feel.

Wendy   Don't give me this, Sonny.

Sonny   One thing I know is, I've known you all my life. I always thought . . .

Wendy   Don't flatter yourself . . .

Sonny   I don't need this!

Wendy   Yes you do!

Sonny   You're no better than me!

Pause.

Wendy   Today I was washing this bloke's hair. He reached up and squeezed my tit. My right . . . Not hard – just a squeeze. I didn't do anything. He abused me, but I – I wasn't . . .

Sonny   Who is he? Tell me who he is – I'll kill him.

Wendy   You abuse me.

Sonny   I've never laid a finger on you.

Wendy   The way you talk to me, the way you look at me . . . I don't know why I came here, Sonny. I pretend I care what Teresa says. I pretend that my mum hates me. I pretend like a fucking kid!

A beat.

When I picked up the phone I thought — Shit, go to the pub, get out — have a laugh. No. With you, Sonny? I must be thick. I must have been in a right sodding dream.

Scene Five

Val *and* **Nick** *sit on the sofa in the flat.* **Val** *has a wrapped present.*

Val   You didn't have to, Nick.

Nick   It's all right. My treat. Plonk's in the fridge.

Val   Never had a birthday like it.

Nick   Go on, open it.

Val *opens the present. She takes out a pink jumper.*

Val   Oh, it's lovely, Nick.

She kisses him.

Oh, look, you've only gone and left the price tag on, you berk!

Nick   I haven't.

Val   You have. Look. Nine ninety-nine.

Nick   Show us?

Val   I thought I was worth more than that to you, you dirty bugger!

Nick *kisses* **Val** *on the cheek.*

Nick   Course you are.

Val   Thanks, Nick.

Nick   So where's the cake and candles?

Val   You must be joking. The day my Charlie and Sonny manage to get me a birthday cake I'll run up and down the block naked. I'll tell you something, Nick. I love a sponge, or a gateau, or a fruit pie, or cream, but the day I bake my own bloody birthday cake is the day I pack it in.

Charlie (*offstage*)   Val!

Nick   Christ . . .

Charlie (*offstage*)   Val! Val – make us a cup of tea love! I'm gasping . . .

Pause.

Nick   I didn't know Charlie was here . . .

Val   He came out this morning . . .

Nick   You could've said. We could've been . . . doing anything . . .

Val   It's all right, Nick – Can't get out of bed unless I help him . . .

Charlie (*offstage*)   Val! Are you making that tea? Val!

A beat.

I don't know. I'm in hospital in agony. I'm putting up with all the geriatrics and the nurses.

Nick and **Val** *smile.*

Charlie (*offstage*)   Not a smiling face on that ward in all the time I'm in there. And you look forward to the comfort of being in your own home – and you get out and your own wife can't even be bothered to make you a cup of tea . . . Val . . . Val!

Val   All right, Charlie!

Pause.

Nick   Where's Sonny?

Val   Don't know – but I think he must have gone to meet a girl because he stank of Charlie's Old Spice.

Pause.

Charlie's mate's bringing a wheelchair round tomorrow so he can take him over the park. If that lift's out of order I'll go spare Nick. He's driving me up the bloody wall.

Charlie (*offstage*)   Val!

Val   If you don't shut up, Charlie, I'm going to stick that crutch you've got in there right up your bloody arse!

Nick *grins and sits up a bit on the sofa.*

Nick   I feel a bit uncomfortable here, Val. I think I'm sitting on something.

He reaches behind his backside and pulls out a crumpled card.

It's a birthday card – I'm sorry, Val. It's a bit creased.

Val   Give us it here. It's Sonny's card.

Nick   Can I read it?

Val   If you want.

Nick (*reads aloud*)   Dear Mum. Have a really pucker day and get pissed.

Val   I don't know why he said get pissed. Even when Charlie's here he doesn't take me anywhere.

Nick   Love from Sonny. Kiss, kiss, kiss. He's spelt love wrong!

Val   He may not be able to spell it but he means it.

Nick   Thought you had problems with Sonny?

Val   He's a bloody sod but he's never hurt me.

Nick   The way he talks to you?

Val   His way of carrying on. Doesn't mean it – just does it. His protection I think. There are only two things in the world Sonny really cares about – his cricket and his mum. I worry about Sonny.

Pause.

Last Friday, Nick . . . It's not the first time he's come home with blood . . .

Nick   I told you, Val.

Pause.

Sonny can take care of himself.

Val   Can he?

A beat.

I see him looking out of the window across London. I just think it would take so little to make him push it open and jump.

Nick   Not Sonny.

Val   I know, Nick. I know.

Pause.

I know.

Pause.

You know the council have painted some of the prefab squares on the blocks red and blue.

Pause.

Nick   You're all right. You've got Sonny and Charlie.

Val   Liberal council that is. Looks like bloody Lego. Looks like it could fall apart so easily.

Nick   You've got some money coming in. Could be a lot worse.

Val   Funny. Things can always be worse. It's just how much you can stand.

Pause.

You know, Nick, however big or small a slice of cake I have, I still feel sick. If I stuff myself silly it's too sickly and I'm bloated. If I just take a bite I feel hungrier and hungrier till I feel mad.

Nick   (*laughing*)   P'raps you should stop eating cake?

Val *laughs and reaches over for a kiss.*

Val   P'raps I should.

Val *and* **Nick** *kiss, easily, lovingly.* **Charlie** *appears in the entrance into the room. He's dressed only in a dirty old vest and Y-front*

underpants. He hobbles forward and goes to speak but notices **Nick**
and **Val** *kissing, who don't notice him.* **Charlie** *turns away.*

Scene Six

Sonny *sits on the sofa in the flat reading a copy of the* Sun. *A doorbell
rings offstage.* **Sonny** *gets up and goes out to answer it. Pause.* **Sonny**
and **Nick** *enter.* **Sonny** *sits down and picks up the paper again.*

Nick   I got it, Sonny. I fucking got it, didn't I!

Sonny   When do you start?

Nick   Monday. Got to be at the depot by six o'clock
though. Jesus, last time I was up that early I was tripping my
tits off.

Sonny   Won't be doing that any more then, now you're
working.

Nick   Oh no. I might not be out as much but I'm still going
to trip out. Never know, Sonny — might be able to get some
Charlie now I'm earning. You watch, we'll soon be doing
lines of coke through fifty-pound notes.

Sonny   Off bin-money?

Nick   It's a start, Sonny.

Sonny   Yeah, great.

Nick   Do what?

Sonny   I said great.

Nick   You sound fucked off. What's up?

Sonny   Nothing.

Nick   No, come on, we're mates.

Sonny   Are we?

Nick   What's that supposed to mean?

Sonny   What do you think it means?

Nick   I don't know? What's the matter? Look, Sonny . . .

Pause.

For fuck's sake, Sonny, tell me what's wrong?

No reply.

Just leave this shit out, Sonny!

Sonny (*showing him page three*)   Tits on that.

Nick (*ripping the paper away*)   Don't fuck with me, Sonny. What is this moody bollocks?

Sonny   Nothing.

Nick   You ain't fucking jealous, are you?

Sonny   Piss off, Nick.

Nick   What is it then?

Pause.

Sonny   I know you've been seeing her.

Nick   What . . .

Sonny   Tell me the truth.

Nick   I don't . . .

Sonny   I'll kill you.

Nick   Sonny . . .

Sonny   She reckons you haven't but I know you've been fucking her.

Nick   I couldn't help it.

Sonny   Oh yeah . . .

Nick   Val's always so nice . . .

Sonny   What?

Nick   Val . . .

Sonny   Val?

Nick   I . . .

Sonny   My mum?

Pause.

Wendy's told me . . .

Nick   But I thought – Val . . .

Sonny   No. No.

He sits in stunned silence.

The jumper and card. From you – the jumper and card. I thought it was strange.

Nick   I'm sorry . . .

Sonny   Shit, you still left the price tag on. Nine fucking ninety-nine – is that what she was worth?

Nick   I didn't mean it.

Sonny   What, leave the tag on? You've been fucking my mum, you cunt! Aaaaarrrrgh – I could fucking kill you now! You bastard!

Nick   Sonny.

Sonny (*on his feet*)   Don't fucking speak to me. I don't want to hear it!

Pause. He continues less angrily.

We're meant to be mates. I trusted you. I don't trust anyone. I trusted you. Shit, I would die for you, you cunt. I would die for you!

Long pause.

So, Nicky-boy, how long's it been going on?

Nick   It's only happened twice.

Sonny   Only! What's the matter, sack of shit, was she?

Pause.

Nick   No.

Sonny   Aaaah you cunt!

He lunges at **Nick** *and throttles him. They fall onto the floor and* **Nick** *gasps for breath. They struggle.* **Sonny** *slaps* **Nick** *around the face.*

Don't fucking cry!

He gets up.

Fucking bollocks, bollocks! Get up, get out! Go on fuck off!

Nick *exits quickly. Long pause.* **Sonny** *picks up the* Sun *and sits down on the sofa. Pause as he reads.* **Val** *enters with two bags of shopping.*

Val   All right, Sonny. Put the kettle on for me, would you, love.

She goes offstage into the kitchen. We hear her voice.

I saw Nick on his way downstairs. He ran straight past me. You haven't been on that funny stuff, have you? Nick didn't look very well.

She wanders back in.

D'you want some cake, Sonny? It's victoria sponge – I know you like victoria sponge. I got two in Tesco's. Special discount. Sonny? I don't know, you and your moods.

She goes back into the kitchen.

I know where you get your moods. It's your father's side of the family. Your uncle's just the same. I saw Nick's mum in Tesco's. She said Nick got a job at the depot.

She comes back in with a tray, two mugs of tea and the cake cut in two.

Here you are love. I cut you a bit of cake anyway. I know you like your victoria sponge. Are you all right, Sonny? Sonny? Sod you – I'll eat it then.

She eats half of the cake very quickly punctuated by gulps of tea. Her mouth is half full.

Are you sure you don't want any cake?

She carries on chewing.

I don't know if I can manage all this, eyes bigger than my belly. I saw Nick's mum in Tesco's . . .

Sonny Yeah, I know.

Val She said Nick's got a job at the rubbish tip. You didn't say anything about it, Sonny.

Sonny No.

Val You are in a funny mood. Too much of that pot makes your brains go funny.

Pause.

I like Nick. You should try and take after him a bit more, Sonny. It's a wonder you hadn't thought of going down that rubbish tip. Whatever else, people always have rubbish to get rid of. Now there is a business that's never out of work and I bet there are some good bits and pieces thrown out that you can pick up. You know your Aunt Vi. Well, she knew a bloke who was on the dustbins. When she was courting with him you'll never guess what he found — a solid diamond ring! Amongst all that filth and muck — a diamond ring. He had it valued — guess how much it was worth? Two thousand quid, in 1969! Didn't tell anyone he'd found a ring. He told them all he'd won the pools. He paid everyone in his block of flats a week's rent and treated your Aunt Vi to a weekend in Blackpool. I don't think your Aunt Vi was very grateful. I think she thought she was off to sunny Spain.

Pause. She starts to hum 'Viva España' then laughs at herself.

Bloody hell, Charlie never has any of that luck. And I'll tell you, Sonny — I wouldn't mind Blackpool. I'd like to see the lights.

Pause.

I've got a new cleaning job, Sonny — you'll never guess where. Harrods! Oh, you should see it, Sonny, it's beautiful. Beautiful — and the toilets, you've never seen anything like it in your life, Sonny. Lovely tiles. I don't expect to say this about any other lav, but I would have those tiles in my kitchen.

Pause.

Pokey little thing that kitchen is. Can't swing a cat.

Pause.

Two of us who've got jobs today. Me and Nick. You see, you can get a job if you really want one, Sonny. You should do what what's-his-name said. Erm ... You know, Norman ... Looks like a bit of a skeleton with a bald head. Anyway, you should get on your bike. Go out and look. There's nothing wrong with good honest hard work. We've done it in the past and we'll do it again. Now I'll tell you what's wrong with this country, Sonny. We have become mollycoddled. The immigrants are the only people used to hard work. Now whatever you say about the Pakistanis, they know how to work. What do I get for my cleaning? One-fifty, two quid an hour. Not much. But it gets me by. I'm not proud. I don't mind not having much. People like us have always been poor. But I know I'm honest – and I've never needed to take drugs. You lot have got it made, Sonny, sitting on your backside claiming the dole and going out thieving. Now I know you do it. I don't know how you've got the cheek sometimes. D'you know, Sonny, that a pair of jeans you put in the laundry bag last week still had the labels all over it. And it was a size forty-two, so I know it wasn't yours. Anyhow, I know you haven't got the money to afford to buy them.

Pause.

I don't know what's the matter with you, Sonny. I did my best for you and look how you've turned out – and the temper sometimes. It's like putting up with a bloody kid. And that mug you smashed in the week – that was my royal wedding souvenir that was, and I only got it out cos there wasn't a clean one in the kitchen to be had. You don't lift a finger – and the habits ... That was my favourite mug. The only thing I had, Sonny. Your bloody father chucked the scrapbook out with the rubbish. That wedding was beautiful – beautiful, Sonny. Charles and Di. That beautiful dress, beautiful. Didn't I cry – Didn't I cry, Sonny ...

Sonny *stands*.

Val   Where are you going?

Sonny   To the pub.

Val   What for?

Sonny   I'm going to get arseholed.

Val   Funny mood you're in.

Sonny   I want to see Nick.

Scene Seven

Wendy *and* **Teresa** *sit on the park bench in one stage area.* **Val** *and* **Charlie** *sit on the sofa in the other stage area.* **Val** *has a tray with a cake and* **Charlie** *has his foot in plaster and reads the* Sun.

Teresa   I can't believe it.

Wendy   Neither can I.

Val   There's some cake here, Charlie.

Pause.

Wendy   I feel sick thinking about it.

Pause.

Charlie   I'm not hungry.

Wendy   And now to top it all off that wanker at the salon has sacked me. Two days off, Trese – that's all I had. When do I ever have a day off?

Val   When are we going to see the baby?

Pause.

Teresa   It's hard to take in, Wendy.

Val   The baby's been born four days, Charlie . . .

Wendy   I know.

Val   She's my sister.

Pause.

Wendy   I feel numb. It's my fault – I know it's my fault, Trese.

Val   Are you going to eat any of this cake?

Charlie   No.

Val   I made it specially. It's got cream on it – and flake. Flake on top as well . . .

Charlie   I don't want your fucking cake!

Pause.

Wendy   He cut that poor bastard's face to pieces.

Pause.

Teresa   I've come on, Wend . . .

Val   I'll eat it then – I'll eat it.

Teresa   I've come on . . . No more worries eh, Wend . . . Wendy?

Val   Cake.

Teresa   They're all monsters, Wendy . . .

Val   Cake.

Teresa   Sonny's a fucking monster . . .

Val *breaks off handfuls of the cake which she disturbingly stuffs in her mouth. The tears roll down her face.*

Wendy   We're all monsters, Trese.

Val   I want to eat cake.

A Week with Tony

For Uncle John and Michael Willis

A Week with Tony was first performed by the Steam Industry at the Finborough Theatre, London, on 19 June 1996. The cast was as follows:

Annie	Di Langford
Elizabeth	Celia Robertson
Ursula	Rachel Kemp
Amelia	Emma Pallant
Joseph	Oscar Pearce
Henry	Theo Fraser Steele
Guy	Paul Ebsworth
Malcolm	Robert Thorogood
Nicholas	Robert Donald
Jacqui	Carrie Thomas
Tony	Ric Morgan
Hayes/Roger	Keith Hazemore
Penny	Helen Higham

Directed by Mark Ravenhill
Designed by Christopher Oram
Lighting by Hartley Kemp
Sound by David Payne

Characters

Tony, *sales representative for a computer firm. Fifty-four.*
Penny, *Tony's boss in Computer Sales. Thirty-one.*
Roger, *salesman and Tony's friend at work. Fifties.*
Annie, *Tony's ex-wife. Not working. Fifty-one.*
Elizabeth, *Tony's daughter. Not working. Twenty-six.*
Ursula, *Elizabeth's friend, works in PR. Twenty-seven.*
Amelia, *younger friend of Elizabeth, works in PR, member of the Christian Conservatives. Twenty-two.*
Henry, *Elizabeth's fiancé, stockbroker. Twenty-seven.*
Guy, *Conservative party agent, Amelia's partner. Thirty-two.*
Malcolm, *Henry's best friend, director of a city firm trading Yen, and Tory councillor. Twenty-six.*
Nicholas, *Henry's father, Conservative constituency party chairman, director of a prestigious merchant bank and on the board of a PR company. Fifty-seven.*
Jacqui, *Tony's partner, former mistress and city-based PA. Thirty-four.*
Hayes, *clergyman to conduct the wedding. Fifties.*
Joseph, *Tony's godson. Twenty-four.*

Setting

The play is set in a hot summer week in 1996. The weather is very sunny until a storm breaks on the second Saturday halfway through Act Two.

A Week with Tony was inspired by Trevor Griffiths' original plan to make six 'Tory Stories' for the BBC. In the end only one, *Country*, was made. Here is another – for the stage.

Act One

Scene One

Saturday evening. The lower level bar at the Barbican centre, London. **Annie** *enters, looks around, checks her watch and sighs. Pause.* **Elizabeth**, *her daughter, enters.*

Annie   You're late . . .

Elizabeth   I know – I've been looking for you for the last half an hour. Shall we get a drink?

Annie   No. Let's wait till some of the others are here.

Elizabeth   I hate the Barbican! I hate it, I hate, I hate it! I can never find were I'm going!

Annie   How was your day?

Elizabeth   Michelle Frank's being so difficult about the design for my dress. I told her from the start that I want something classic but she's determined to make a flash of it . . .

Annie   I know, dear.

Elizabeth   And we're having fittings and things for Ursula and Amelia on Thursday. I know Michelle'll be difficult . . .

Annie   It'll be fine . . .

Elizabeth   And Henry's bought a video. 'Plan Your Perfect Wedding.' It's with that woman who does the holiday programmes. Oh, you know . . .

Pause. She thinks hard, clicking her fingers.

It'll come to me . . .

Annie   Judith Chalmers?

Elizabeth   Judith Chalmers! Yes . . .

A beat.

Annie   So where's Henry?

Elizabeth   God knows . . .

Annie   How much d'you think it'll all cost then?

Elizabeth   What?

Annie   The whole thing – the whole wedding. Have you got a final figure for your father?

Elizabeth   Including the honeymoon?

Annie   Just what your father's paying for?

Elizabeth   I don't know – Forty thousand pounds, give or take a thousand or two . . .

Annie   That much? I never realised . . .

Elizabeth   Where've you been living for the last year? This is going to be the best and biggest wedding, Mum.

Pause.

Annie   I never realised he made so much money from computers.

Elizabeth   Oh, it's not that . . .

Annie   Well, where's he getting the money from then?

Elizabeth   You know – the policies . . .

Annie   What policies?

Elizabeth   Well, he told me he's been paying into them for years . . .

Annie   Well, it's the first I've heard of it – They would've been mentioned in our settlement . . .

Elizabeth   Daddy would hardly've dragged my wedding money through the divorce courts. Would you've wanted to contest that money?

Annie   No, of course not . . . But I think he would've been required by law to declare those assets . . .

Elizabeth   Maybe he cashed them and tucked the money away somewhere. Anyway he'd've had to hide it away when the receivers were called in . . .

Annie   But money like that doesn't simply disappear . . .

Elizabeth   Of course it does, all the time. Look at the city. Henry and Malcolm are full of stories . . .

Annie *nods in agreement. Pause.*

Elizabeth   You've said it yourself – Daddy's a stickler for planning. (*A beat.*) He's meant to be coming tonight . . .

Annie   Is he?

Ursula *enters. She looks stunning.*

Elizabeth   Hello, darling . . . (*They embrace.*)

Annie   Hello, Ursula. (**Annie** *is embraced in turn.*)

Ursula   Sorry I'm late . . .

Annie   We've only just got here . . .

Ursula   Terrible trouble finding the place – And I got harangued by a tramp I trod on coming out of Moorgate . . .

Elizabeth   How awful.

Ursula   But what a stupid place to sit? Haven't you ordered a drink?

Elizabeth   Not yet.

Ursula   I've spent all afternoon chatting up this man in oil . . .

Annie   Is he nice?

Ursula   He's American – Very fat, Lizzie.

Elizabeth   Oh, why bother?

Ursula   Money, darling. I'm doing the PR for his company's new petrol station gifts. Yukky little teddy bears . . .

Annie   Splendid . . .

Ursula   Over here for the week, Lizzy – As long as he doesn't try and touch me up I don't mind taking a cigar wrapper off with my teeth and leaving some lipstick on the tip . . .

Elizabeth   You are naughty, Ursula.

Ursula   He's taking me shopping tomorrow.

Elizabeth   Is he card friendly?

Ursula   Of course. Wallet full of gold cards and getting them out all of the time . . .

Elizabeth   I don't know what Henry'd do without his cards. He's too badly organised to manage cash . . .

Ursula   Still, you'll make use of the working-class thrift in your genes when you're married . . .

Elizabeth   Excuse me? – Your father's from Liverpool . . .

Ursula   Do I look like I'm related to Cilla Black? Of course your father's relatives are still eating jellied eels. (*She laughs mockingly.*) Have you booked a disco for the wedding yet?

Elizabeth   You'd like it, Ursula – Always up for a slow dance and a grope, Ursula is, Mummy . . .

Ursula   That's about your level, Lizzie . . .

Annie   Girls . . .

Elizabeth   You've cruised the singles bars in your time . . .

Annie   Stop it . . .

Elizabeth   Not to mention singles night at Asda . . .

Annie   Now then . . .

Ursula   You bitch, Lizzy . . .

Annie   I think that's quite enough.

Elizabeth   We're just playing, aren't we, Ursula?

Ursula   Yes.

Pause.

Annie   Malcolm'll be jealous of your oil man, Ursula.

Ursula   Oh – screw Malcolm.

Elizabeth   Well, traditionally that's what you're . . .

Annie   I think he's all right . . .

Elizabeth   You would. Well, if you're not having the best man what about the chief usher?

Ursula   Joseph?

Annie   Now don't start on Joey ...

Elizabeth   He is strange ... D'you think he's gay?

Annie   Elizabeth!

Ursula   I don't think so.

She winks at **Elizabeth**.

I think he's probably a bit kinky ...

Annie   Joseph?!

Ursula   I can tell, Annie. I can tell. I saw him coming out of the loo at the engagement party doing up his belt. It's the way they do up their straps – always gives it away ...

Elizabeth *laughs.*

Ursula   I met this guy from Dusseldorf a couple of years back. Fiddled with his belt the whole time. Went back to his place for coffee – Crikey – It was like the London Dungeons – Not that I've ever been.

Pause. **Ursula** *and* **Elizabeth** *exchange a look and smile.*

Annie   Not Joseph ...

Amelia *enters. Although a few years younger she is a good friend of* **Elizabeth**.

Amelia   Joseph? Is he coming?

Annie   Now?

Ursula *and* **Elizabeth** *erupt with laughter.*

Annie   Girls!

Amelia   What's so funny?

Annie   Nothing, they're being silly. (*A beat.*) I'm going to order a couple of bottles.

Ursula   Red please ...

Elizabeth   Red's fine ...

Annie   Well, I don't know where everyone's got to but we're going to be late ...

She exits.

Amelia   What was all that about?

Ursula   We were just winding her up about Joseph ...

Amelia   How are you?

Amelia *embraces* **Elizabeth**, *but not* **Ursula**.

Elizabeth   I'm fine ...

Amelia   Joseph's lovely ...

Elizabeth   Yes – and much nicer than Guy – Amelia ...

Ursula   Why are you so late, Amelia?

Amelia   I couldn't find you – I was upstairs somewhere at first ...

Ursula   You weren't praying then?

Elizabeth   Ursula ...

Pause.

Amelia   I ran into your father this morning.

Elizabeth   Lucky you. I've been calling him for days.

Amelia   He said he's coming to the barbecue tomorrow ...

Elizabeth   He's meant to be here tonight ...

Ursula   It's going to be awful, I know it ...

Amelia   Is Joseph coming tonight?

Elizabeth   Yes ...

Joseph *enters unnoticed by* **Amelia**. *He is* **Annie**'s *godson and looks quite trendy in his shirt outside his jeans.*

Amelia   He's such a dish ...

Elizabeth
Ursula } Hello, Joseph ...

Joseph   Hi – sorry I'm late ...

Amelia   Hello, Joseph . . .

Joseph (*kissing* **Amelia** *on the cheek*)   Hello, Milly – How are you, darling?

Amelia   Fine.

Elizabeth   Did you get lost?

Joseph   No – I've been here before . . .

Henry *enters. He's* **Elizabeth**'*s fiancé, is handsome and wears a very well cut pinstripe suit.*

Henry   Hello, everyone . . . (*Kissing* **Elizabeth**.) Sorry I'm late . . .

Elizabeth   Everyone seems to have got lost –

Amelia   Did you get lost, Henry?

Henry   No – I was early actually – I went over to the South Bank by mistake . . .

Ursula   RSC, darling . . .

Annie *re-enters with* **Guy**. **Guy** *wears a suit slightly too small for him, and carries six wine glasses.* **Annie** *has two bottles of red wine and two more glasses.* **Guy** *kisses* **Amelia** *on the cheek.*

Guy   Hello, Mills . . .

Annie   Hello, Joseph – This is more like it . . . We've just got time to have a drink . . .

Ursula *takes one bottle, and the two glasses from* **Annie**, *which she fills for herself and* **Elizabeth**. **Annie** *starts to fill the glasses* **Guy** *has.* **Amelia** *takes one. As she attempts to pass it to* **Henry**, *he reaches for it – and the glass is knocked up into his face and shirt.*

Elizabeth   Amelia!

Amelia   I'm sorry . . .

Henry   No bother . . .

Amelia   I'm so sorry . . .

Guy   You stupid girl . . .

Joseph   Guy . . .

Henry   No bother at all . . .

Guy (*immediately losing his temper*)   Look what you've done!

Guy's flash of anger silences everyone. People mostly look into their glasses.

Henry   Honestly, Guy, it's no bother at all . . .

Guy   D'you know how much that suit cost! Do you! (*A beat.*) You stupid girl – you're not in a university bar now!

Pause. **Amelia** *is immediately tearful.*

Amelia (*exiting*)   I'm sorry, Henry – I'm sorry . . .

Amelia *exits. Longish pause.*

Guy   I'm sorry.

Henry   Perhaps you should see to Milly?

Guy   She'll be all right. (*A beat.*) She's always crying. You've only got to say the slightest thing, and she's in floods of tears.

Pause. **Henry** *takes another glass of wine from* **Guy** *and is attended to by* **Elizabeth** *with a tissue from her handbag.* **Malcolm** *enters.* **Malcolm** *is* **Henry**'s *best friend.*

Malcolm   Sorry I'm late . . .

Malcolm
Ursula } Terrible trouble finding . . .

Malcolm (*grinning*)   You read my mind, Ursula . . . (*A beat.*) Great outfit – Is it designer?

Ursula *shakes her head.*

Malcolm   Good day today?

Ursula *shakes her head again.*

Malcolm   Not a sore throat, is it? It's the heat you know . . . Hello Henry – don't drop your glass . . .

Henry (*raising his glass*)   Never fear, Malcs ...

Malcolm (*noticing* **Henry**'*s shirt*)   Oh dear – looks like I'm too late ...

Annie   How's your week been, Malcolm?

Malcolm   Oh, you know – made a killing by Wednesday, then lost it all again by Friday – you know how it is ...

Annie   Not like the old days?

Malcolm   No – You talk to some of the older guys still around and the stories they tell are incredible. I think champagne and caviar was compulsory. You got the tail-end, didn't you, Henry?

Henry   Not really – I started in eighty-nine.

Elizabeth   D'you think those days'll ever come back?

Annie (*at the same time as* **Ursula**)   No ...

Ursula   Yes ...

Pause.

Elizabeth   Well – whatever happens, Henry and I are going to get the biggest and best start.

This breaks the ice a little. Only **Guy** *doesn't smile, which is noticed.*

Henry   You know she's watched *Four Weddings* fifty-three times, haven't you darling?

Elizabeth   Henry!

Annie   Are you all right, Guy?

Guy   I've just had a bad day.

Annie   Have a drink.

Guy   No, I'm driving.

Pause.

I've just had to deal with something very difficult today. I was called into the office – on a Saturday – to see this old man – Apparently one of the councillors in our group promised

he'd do something about his argument with a neighbour –
about an extension . . .

Malcolm   Well, it wasn't me . . .

Guy   In nineteen ninety-two actually. He's been in
correspondence for all that time and nothing's actually been
done. And to make things worse, Simon Robinson – who
promised the old boy, lost his seat last time round. I tried to
explain but he went on and on and on – you know the sort of
thing, going on about how we've betrayed them –

Ursula (*sarcastically*)   How terrible . . .

Guy (*a beat*)   Then he gets out a Victoria Cross.

Pause.

Elizabeth   Was it genuine?

Guy   I don't know . . .

Malcolm (*making a show of this*)   Would you give me the
details, Guy? – I'll see to it on Monday . . .

Elizabeth   They're worth a lot of money, you know, and I
bet it's not insured. A lot of pensioners don't bother . . .

Annie   I suspect it's a lot more to do with money than a
lack of effort . . .

Pause.

Ursula   D'you really think that there are any poor people
any more?

Annie   Of course.

Ursula   I don't think so. I mean, you see one or two tramps
kicking around, but I really do think, the television blows it
all out of proportion – especially the BBC . . .

Nicholas, **Henry**'s *father, enters. He is very jolly, but detects the
reflective mood. He has a bottle of champagne and a glass in hand.*

Henry   Hello.

Nicholas   Is everyone all right?

Malcolm   We were just talking about the BBC . . .

Ursula   Reds, Trots and commies the lot of them . . .

Nicholas   Well, I don't know – There was a time when you could go on a night out with a party from the club and the most political things got was a moan about a tax return – We're becoming as obsessed with politics as the Labour party . . . Are we missing someone? Where's Amelia?

Guy   She's not here – She's not very well.

Nicholas   That's a damn shame.

Elizabeth   Daddy's not here yet . . .

Nicholas   Oh – he couldn't come – he's seeing the vicar tonight . . .

Malcolm   Lucky we're not paying for the tickets . . .

Ursula   Who has paid for them?

Nicholas   Some Japanese bugger. We've done a lot of PR for them over here . . . (*Stretching out a hand to* **Joseph**.) Hello there – We met at the engagement party –

Joseph (*shaking hands*)   Yes – Thanks for the ticket . . .

Nicholas   Ever seen a *Julius Caesar*?

Joseph   Yes – I go to the theatre quite regularly . . .

Nicholas   I like to stick to Shakespeare – good for the soul and always a safe bet for a night out. Good God – I got taken along to see a play in Chelsea and I was quite shocked. All eye-gouging and buggery and not five minutes from the King's Road!

Henry   Sounds like school, Dad . . .

Nicholas   Stick to Shakespeare I say – He was a Tory, you know?

Joseph *smiles politely.*

Nicholas   Look, I got some bubbly – Get the evening going . . .

Annie Well done, Nicky . . .

Nicholas *immediately cracks open the bottle and fills the glasses, with 'there you go's, 'hello's and plenty of good humour.*

Elizabeth Shouldn't we be going in?

Annie Well, I haven't heard any announcement . . .

Finishing, **Nicholas** *speaks to the assembled group.*

Nicholas Well, could I just say that my son, Henry, and my future daughter-in-law, Elizabeth's wedding is going to be the first constituency wedding in ten years and I'm jolly well looking forward to it!

There is laughter and general approval from the assembled group.

And since you mentioned politics, Malcolm – that rabble in Westminster might not be helping us to pull together – but if there's one thing that's going to pull our constituency together and unite our Tory party it's a traditional English wedding . . .

Annie Hear, hear . . .

Nicholas Let's have a toast?

Henry Not like you to bandy about a toast, Dad?

Nicholas What?

Henry Last time you toasted anything was Major in ninety-two. We didn't even get one when we got engaged.

Nicholas Didn't you?

Henry No.

Nicholas Well, not to worry – we're having one now. 'To Henry and Elizabeth' . . .

All (*raising their glasses*) To Henry and Elizabeth . . .

Henry And the Japanese bugger!

All (*with laughter*) And the Japanese bugger!

Scene Two

Saturday evening. **Jacqui**, **Tony**'s *girlfriend, wanders slowly across the stage perfectly happy in the peaceful atmosphere of a church.* **Tony** *enters and smiles but it isn't really responded to by* **Jacqui**.

Tony   Jacqui?

Jacqui   Sorry?

Tony   You haven't seen the vicar?

Jacqui   No.

Tony   Are we early?

Jacqui   Yes. Ten minutes to go yet ...

Tony   Oh ...

Jacqui   Nice church, isn't it? (**Tony** *nods.*) I like the feel of a church.

Tony   Really?

Jacqui   You know, the smell. I mean, I wouldn't want to go every Sunday – I just like ...

Tony   The quiet?

Jacqui   Yes.

Pause.

I did wonder if there might be a choir ...

Tony   Tonight?

Jacqui   Evensong – something like that.

Pause.

When I was a little girl I got separated from my mother in the street – I was crying – And I found my way to a church. I know it sounds like a fairy tale but I did. And I felt a hand on my shoulder – and I turned – and I was scared – and I cried – But he just – he just put his finger on his lips – and pushed open the door. This sound – like magic – the choir singing, drifted out of the church. (*A beat.*) For years, you know, I thought that was what happened when you died and went to heaven. Someone slowly opened an oak door and that sound pulled you in.

Pause.

It took me a long time to work out the tune. I realised when I watched the cup final with my brothers, and I heard 'Abide With Me'. It was like someone threw up the shutters.

Pause.

I'm sorry. I'm sorry – I've been prattling on.

Tony   I love listening to you. Annie never talked like that.

A beat.

Jacqui   Elizabeth rang again this afternoon. (*A beat.*) You've got to speak to her, Tony.

Tony.   I will tomorrow . . . I'll speak to her and I'll arrange a time when we can speak alone and I can explain . . .

Jacqui *shakes her head. Pause.*

Tony   Are you coming with me tomorrow?

Jacqui *shakes her head again.*

Tony   Why?

Jacqui   You know very well that Annie's going to be there . . .

Tony   I'd just like you to be there with me – I'd just like some support . . .

Jacqui   Well, why don't you speak to Annie – Why don't you tell her – Why don't you ask her for support, you talk about her enough . . .

Tony   I'm with you now.

Jacqui   Yeah?

Tony   Yes . . .

Pause.

Jacqui   All I've heard you talk about for the last year is your bloody Annie, and your bloody spoilt daughter, and her bloody wedding.

Tony   All I want is some support . . .

Jacqui   All I want is some support?

Pause.

She's not having a penny of my money for her ridiculous carnival . . .

Tony   I'm not asking you for any money. I'm asking you for a little bit of understanding while I try and get through this.

Jacqui   There is nothing to get through, or get over. You just have to tell your bloody precious daughter and your wife you can't afford it –

Tony   Annie isn't my wife – you're . . .

Jacqui   What? I don't know what any more. I mean, I'm no longer your after-hours fuck, I'm no longer your young bit, and I'm not the woman at the back of the church. What am I, Tony – you tell me . . .

Pause.

Tony   What?

Jacqui   Well, I might as well still play at it.

Tony   Play at what?

Jacqui   Play the game. I have for seven years. (*A beat.*) Everything I say, it's Annie says that, everything I do, it's Annie does that. I don't care about Annie . . .

Tony   I can't just discount . . .

Jacqui   But you can discount what I feel . . .

Tony   Thirty years of my life . . .

Jacqui   You can discount what I want.

Tony   I asked you to come with me this evening because I'm with you now. I'm not married to Annie. If I was . . .

Jacqui   You might as well be . . .

Tony   (*losing his temper*)   If I was I'd have seen the vicar with Annie and Nicholas and Christine last week and I'd be at the bloody theatre with them now!

Pause.

I didn't. I'm not. I'm with you.

Jacqui   I don't know why you bother – you still act as if . . .

Tony   I can't understand this – The way you just turn . . .

Jacqui   When was the last time we went out?

Tony   I don't know . . .

Jacqui   That's right. When was the last time? When I first saw you we did nothing but. We went away, we went to the cinema, we ate out, we ate together, we cooked for each other, we don't do that any more!

Tony   Please, Jacqui, this is a church . . .

Jacqui   I know where I am!

Pause.

Tony   I can't afford to do those things any more . . .

Pause. **Tony**'s *mobile phone rings. He takes it out of his pocket and answers the call.*

Hello . . . Yes, speaking . . .

Realising who's calling, **Tony** *immediately brightens.*

Hello, Geoff, how are you . . . ? Yes . . . you did? You got it?

Pause.

I know, Geoff, I know it's a lot of money . . .

Long pause. **Tony** *listens intently.*

OK, Geoff, no problem . . .

Pause. **Tony** *is now clearly disappointed.*

No . . . Good of you to call, Geoff . . . I know you would . . . I know. (*A beat.*) Give my love to Cheryl . . .

Pause.

Yeah . . . I'll see you at the wedding . . .

Tony *presses a button on the phone and puts it back in his pocket.*
Pause.

Jacqui   Another one of your good mates?

Tony   This isn't fair . . .

Jacqui   Another one who'd really like to help if he could . . .

Tony   For God's sake, Jacqui!

Jacqui   What a shame . . .

Tony   Don't fucking gloat!

Pause.

Jacqui   This is absurd, Tony! You've got to speak to Elizabeth!

Tony   No. (*A beat.*) I'll speak to her when I'm ready . . .

Tony   Well, you're running out of time . . .

Tony   I'll fucking speak to her when I want!

Pause.

Jacqui   Well, this is clear. This is really going to resolve things . . .

Tony   What the hell's this about!

Jacqui   What do you think it's about! I wake up this morning and find bills – red bills – bills that are in my name, addressed to my flat, unpaid, and yet you spend all your time, your energy – everything you have, trying to make some . . . fantasy happen. How am I supposed to feel?

Pause.

You're making me feel like baggage, Tony! I'm not twenty-seven any more. I'm not the woman I was when I met you –

Hayes *enters.*

Hayes   Hello. (*A beat.*) Tony and –

Tony   Jacqui. This is my friend, Jacqui.

Hayes (*shaking hands with* **Tony**, *then* **Jacqui**)   Pleased to meet you.

Tony   And you. I'm sorry. We've both had –

Hayes   I do hope I'm not late, but I thought I heard the phone going off in the vestry . . .

Tony   I think that might have been my mobile phone, Father.

Hayes   Now there's no need to call me Father – David's fine – Honestly.

Tony   Thank you. (*A beat.*) I've switched off my phone . . .

Hayes   I hope so. I should have to put a sign up outside prior to a service before long. They're forever going off in the middle of things here.

Jacqui   It must be very upsetting.

Hayes   It's a shame we weren't able to see you with the rest of the family . . . But, of course, although we used to see families together, it's a changing world now. (*A beat.*) Still – it's wonderful to see a lovely young couple like Henry and Elizabeth making a commitment to marry. So many these days are just content to drift along . . . You must be very proud?

Tony   Yes.

Pause.

Hayes   I understand you work in the computer industry, Tony?

Tony   Yes.

Jacqui   He's a sales rep . . .

Tony   It's a very good business to be in . . .

Jacqui   If you can put up with the crap.

Pause.

Hayes   I see. So you go out directly to people?

Tony   Yeah. I make appointments with interested clients –
businesses, that sort of thing . . .

Hayes   And you try and sell them a computer system . . .

Tony   Things are starting to take off. What with the
internet . . .

Hayes   Yes – some of the younger parishioners have been
saying I should go on-line.

Jacqui   I'm sure you can offer some advice for free, eh,
Tony?

Pause.

Hayes   So d'you have any hobbies in your free time, Tony?

Tony   I try to get a round of golf in when I can.

Hayes   Really?

Tony   Not as much as I used to. I used to play a round
every weekend. Have you ever played, David?

Hayes   Just the once actually. Charity match. I have to say
– I did enjoy getting out in the fresh air. It's lovely being in all
that greenery. Brilliant to have a hobby that enables you to
be in those surroundings . . .

Pause. **Tony** *smiles.*

Tony   You know, it's funny. There is a saying in the game
that golf is a beautiful walk spoilt –

Hayes   What?

Tony   It's true. It's actually as you get better. You improve
your handicap, you get more competitive – and you stop to
notice the surroundings . . .

Jacqui *laughs.* **Tony** *gives her a look. So does* **Hayes**. *Pause.*

Hayes   If you'd like to follow me, my wife's made some sandwiches. Perhaps – you could have a look at my computer?

Hayes *turns and exits.* **Tony** *moves, but notices* **Jacqui** *hasn't followed.*

Tony   You know – you're becoming just like Annie . . .

Jacqui   Well, that's fucking rich!

Tony   Everything I do – everthing I say, you pick over and want to argue about . . . I'm out all day every day of the week, trying to get a living . . .

Jacqui   It's not my fault you fucked up the business! Look at you. Just look at yourself for a minute, Tony. Look what you've become – That stupid accent you've put on . . . When was the last time you saw your family? – Your mother . . .

Tony   But you never liked my family – You stopped me . . .

Jacqui   What's happened to you, Tony!

Hayes *has stepped back into the room.*

Hayes   The sandwiches are just through here. (*A beat.*) Is everything OK?

Tony *nods.* **Jacqui** *smiles.*

Scene Three

Sunday afternoon. Garden party and barbecue at a north London constituency Conservative club. **Elizabeth** *wanders in. She wears a summery dress and takes off her sunglasses as she looks around.* **Guy** *wanders in, casually dressed, smoking a cigar, with a large brandy in hand, followed by* **Malcolm** *wearing tennis gear, and carrying a paper plate piled high with standard garden party and barbecue buffet food.*

Elizabeth   You haven't see my father?

Guy   No –

Malcolm   Last time I saw him he was helping Sir Toby mix the punch –

Elizabeth   Well, if you see my father tell him I'm looking for him . . .

Elizabeth *puts her sunglasses back on and exits.*

Malcolm   Well, what do you want?

Guy   What would you say, Malc, if I said – Sir Toby and did this . . . (*He pats the centre of his chest.*)

Malcolm   I don't know – Has it got anything to do with the Masons?

Guy   No – his heart . . .

Malcolm   Who's heart?

Guy   Sir Toby's!

Malcolm   So?

Guy   And what if I said the name Heseltine . . .

Malcolm   I'd say traitor . . .

Guy   And if I said John Smith . . .

Malcolm   I'd say dead lefty . . .

Guy   Well, add it all up!

Malcolm   I haven't got the faintest idea . . .

Guy   It's Sir Toby! – He's got a heart problem!

Malcolm   Who told you that?

Guy   It's serious – he's going to need surgery . . .

Malcolm   But I've just seen him on the bouncy castle!

Guy   He should be resting – he could drop any minute . . .

Malcolm   But if he dies he might bring down the government!

Tony *enters, again fairly casually dressed, drinking from a wine glass and eating a sausage roll.*

Tony   All right, Malc – Guy. Lovely afternoon.

Guy   Yeah – Lizzy's looking for you ...

Tony   Christ ... (*A beat.*) Are you all right, Malcolm?

Malcolm   I've just heard some appalling news –

Tony   Yes?

Malcolm   It's Sir Toby ...

Tony   What about him ...

Malcolm   It's his heart – he could drop any minute ...

Tony   What?

Guy   It's the word on the street, Tony ...

Malcolm   If he goes we all go – When he pops it – it'll be the end of us all!

Tony   Calm down, Malcolm! (*A beat.*) Now I'm telling you – I've just been speaking to the man and he's as fit as a fiddle! What you've heard's no more than a vicious rumour.

Pause. **Tony** *takes a bite from his sausage roll,* **Malcolm** *tucks into his food, and* **Guy** *pensively smokes and drinks.*

Guy   Did you like the Morris dancers?

Tony   They're not very Finchley.

Guy   They're very Tory though.

Tony   Are they?

Malcolm
Guy } Definitely.

Pause.

Tony   How much d'you think we'll raise this afternoon, Guy?

Guy   I'm hoping for about five hundred quid.

Tony   Is that all?

Guy   Sign of the times, I'm afraid. This sort of bash used to be very *Howard's Way* and *Dynasty* but it's all changed now ...

Malcolm   Well, you could've tried harder with the raffle prizes, Guy. I spotted a tin of Quality Street, a bottle of cheap aftershave and a litre of Lambrusco. Christ, we're the Tory party for God's sake!

Guy   Well, it's not my fault ninety per cent of our membership are over sixty and bring crappy prizes!

Pause.

What a wedding it's going to be, eh, Tony? You do know that Nicholas is trying to get someone important down for it? Of course, as the first constituency wedding for ten years Sir Toby'll be making a speech – if he's up to it ...

Tony   There's nothing wrong with Toby's heart ...

Guy (*smiling*)   I wouldn't bank on it for definite, Tony, but I've heard the name Portillo mentioned ...

Tony   Jesus ...

Malcolm   To us maybe – but to the country – I don't know ...

Guy   What's this? I always thought you dressed to the right, Malcolm?

Malcolm   Well – one has to be realistic about these things. Herr Portillo and Adolf Redwood are hardly adored in the country ...

Ursula *enters. She wears sunglasses and looks stunning.*

Ursula   Hello, boys – what are you doing skulking in the corner?

Guy   Just talking.

Malcolm   Ursula – you look devastating ...

No answer.

I thought we could play tennis?

Ursula *shakes her head.*

Malcolm   Would you like a drink? – Buck's fizz is delicious in this weather ...

Ursula   Get me a vodka, Malcolm.

Malcolm   Ice?

Ursula   Don't ask stupid questions.

Tony *and* **Guy** *intimate they don't want drinks and* **Malcolm** *exits.*

Ursula   Pass me the bucket – please ...

Tony   Malcolm's a nice enough chap ...

Ursula   I'm not interested in nice chaps.

Guy   Not eating, Ursula?

Ursula   I'm having dinner this evening ...

Guy   Really? Who is he?

Ursula   You wouldn't know him – he's in oil.

Tony   Are you all right, Ursula?

Ursula   Your daughter's driving me up the bloody wall about her bloody wedding – and she's determined to put me in peach!

Henry *wanders over drinking. He wears his pinstripe suit, sweats profusely, and has a black eye.*

Tony   Hello, Henry ...

Guy   God, your eye ...

Tony   What's happened?

Henry   Nipped home on the tube to pick up the rest of the smoked salmon, and I had a bit of a scrap as we pulled into Highgate ...

Guy *smiles.*

Henry   Bloody long-haired bugger spilt ash on me and hit me in the eye with a giant-size Toblerone ...

Ursula   Toblerone?

Incredulous silence. **Henry** *is about to answer when his father,* **Nicholas***, enters, again casually dressed.*

Nicholas   Hello, all – I noticed you all over here in the corner . . . Good grief, Henry, what have you done to your eye?

Guy   I think Toblerone's the key . . .

Malcolm *returns with* **Ursula**'s *vodka.*

Malcolm   Toblerone? – Anyone got any?

Henry   It's in my pocket – D'you want a bit, Malcs?

Malcolm   Yes please – Hello, Nicky, enjoying the sun?

Nicholas   Very much. Playing tennis?

Malcolm (*taking the Toblerone from* **Henry**)   Maybe later –

Nicholas   Well, my boy, if I'm not going to get an answer about your eye would you mind fetching me a mineral water?

Henry *turns to exit but pauses to speak to* **Tony***.*

Henry   Oh – when you've got a minute – speak to Lizzie would you, Tony, she's driving me bonkers . . .

Tony *nods and* **Henry** *exits.* **Ursula** *moves across to* **Malcolm** *and takes her drink.*

Ursula   Thank you, Malcolm.

Malcolm (*mouth full*)   Any time.

Nicholas   Shame you missed the *Julius Caesar*, Tony – God, Shakespeare's good for the soul . . .

Ursula   The one in the red toga was terribly good-looking . . .

A slight pause as **Ursula**'s *uncharacteristic comment is noticed.*

Nicholas   How was David Hayes, Tony?

Tony   Fine.

Nicholas   We were at school together, you know – quite the right man to conduct the wedding service, I think. Shame Henry and Lizzy aren't taking advantage of this gorgeous weather to get married – but, of course, the last

seven generations of men in my family have married in the
autumn. One of my forebears served under Disraeli, you
know?

Tony   Really?

Ursula   What's this I've heard about Toby, Nicholas?

Nicholas   What?

Ursula   I heard that he's got a heart problem – practically
about to croak it . . .

Malcolm   I knew it!

Nicholas   Who told you that?

Guy   Well, it's been spreading like wildfire this afternoon –
everyone I've spoken to seems to think . . .

Nicholas   Well, it's a lie.

Malcolm   That's it for us when Sir Toby goes – And don't
think Gorman and those nutters have finished tearing the
party to pieces yet . . .

Tony   Malcolm!

Malcolm   It'll be Canada all over again – we'll be wiped
out. Then those bloody fascists and pinko-wets can fight over
what's left! – But I tell you – I've had it up to here!

Ursula (*coolly*)   Malcolm you're being hysterical. (*A beat.*)
I happen to be a great admirer of Teresa Gorman.

Malcolm (*quieter*)   Well, you're not part of a council group
that's been reduced to single figures, Ursula – then, quite
frankly – you might understand why I'm being so hysterical.

Guy   Well, if there's a by-election we'll struggle to keep a
hold on this seat –

Tony   What do you mean, Guy? We'd win – we'd win –

Guy   Come on, Tony – You're not out on the doorsteps as
much as you used to be.

Tony   What are you saying – I don't have that sort of time
any more . . .

Guy   I'm not questioning your loyalty – I'm just saying you're a bit out of touch –

Tony   Well, you're hardly being loyal acting like this, Guy – spreading rumours about Sir Toby – saying we're going to lose. Where's the loyalty in that, Guy, you're supposed to be our agent!

Malcolm   They'll all be down here, Jon Snow, Jeremy Paxman – the constituency where the death of an MP led to the disintegration of the Tory party as we know it! – We'll all be interviewed!

Ursula   Really?

Pause.

Well, I don't see what difference it'll make if we do get kicked out. What you're talking about will never happen, Malcolm. We'll come back in five years with – I don't know – Prime Minister Lilley, Chancellor Portillo, and Foreign Secretary Redwood – that's my team . . .

Tony, **Guy** *and* **Malcolm** *speak at the same time.*

Tony   Don't be ridiculous – people'll never wear it!

Guy   Well, Central Office won't be happy with that leadership!

Malcolm   Brilliant – the Fourth Reich in London!

Nicholas (*quietly but with authority*)   That's quite enough.

Pause.

Now I'm chairman of this constituency party and I won't tolerate this bickering. All this rumour and insinuation – you're behaving as badly as the government who're messing things up for us!

Pause.

Now let me be quite clear about this – Sir Toby has not got a heart problem, he is in completely good health – and in fact his doctor – to whom I've switched for treatment – remarked to me only this week how fit Sir Toby is for his age . . . Now

whatever happens nationally – at Westminster, we will
continue to do our best and we will have no more of this
poisonous and untrue gossip.

Annie, **Henry** *and* **Amelia** *enter laughing and in high spirits, not
noticing the serious mood of the group.* **Annie** *and* **Amelia** *drink
wine and* **Henry** *has an ice cream.*

Henry   Bugger – I forgot your water, Dad.

Nicholas   No bother, Henry.

Henry   I'll go and get it for you ...

Annie (*laughing*)   Good God – you all look depressed!

Henry *and* **Amelia** *laugh. No one else does. A beat.*

Malcolm   If only Margaret was still in charge.

Guy   I think every true Conservative was sorry the day that
she went.

A beat.

Malcolm   I don't mind admitting – I'm proud of it, to be
frank. Watching her pull away from Number Ten – I cried.

Ursula   Ahhhhh ...

This is ignored by the group lost in thought.

Guy   I was in the office when I heard she resigned ...
Phones started to ring like mad and as soon as Jean answered
one call she burst into tears.

Pause.

Nicholas   You know – I think I'll have some of that
magnificent buffet of yours, Henry. (*A beat.*) You know the
restaurant's going to be success, I know it will –

Tony   What restaurant?

Henry   Dad's setting me and Lizzie up in a restaurant,
Tony ...

Annie   It's very generous, Tony ...

Nicholas   Well, the honeymoon doesn't seem much of a gift. Henry's a wizard in the kitchen and your Lizzie's degree's in business and finance . . .

Henry   Be good to get out of the city . . .

Annie   It'll be terrific.

A beat.

Nicholas   Come on, Henry – let's go and get some food. (*Exiting with* **Henry**.) You didn't tell me what happened to your eye . . .

Henry   Bloody hippy, Dad – I think he was on drugs . . .

They exit.

Annie   All right, Tony.

Tony   Someone could've told me about the restaurant . . .

Annie   We've not spoken to you for weeks – Lizzie's been trying to get in touch . . . (*A beat.*) D'you remember where we were when we heard about Margaret, Tony?

Tony   Of course . . .

Annie   Coffee in Harvey Nichols – the Guardian reader in the corner bought champagne – and we just sat in silence . . .

Tony   I have to go, Annie – I'm sorry . . .

Tony *starts to go out.*

Annie   Speak to Elizabeth before you go – there are things she wants to discuss . . .

Tony (*exiting*)   I'll call her in the week . . .

Annie (*following*)   Tony!

Tony *exits followed by* **Annie**. **Ursula** *goes to follow.*

Malcolm   Are you going?

Ursula *nods and* **Malcolm** *moves close and catches her arm.*

Malcolm   I'm sorry I was short with you earlier, Ursula . . .

Ursula   Not at all, Malcolm. It was quite exciting seeing the bull stirring within.

Malcolm   Really?

Ursula   I have to shoot, Malcolm – I'm eating out later ...

Malcolm   Oh? – We can go together, if you like, Ursula?

Ursula   Are you in oil?

Malcolm (*grinning*)   Not literally ...

Ursula *shakes her head and steps towards* **Guy** *and* **Amelia**.

Ursula   Goodbye, Guy. Goodbye, Amelia.

Guy   See you.

Ursula (*turning back*)   Goodbye, Malcolm.

Ursula *mischievously runs a finger across* **Malcolm**'s *chest as she exits.*

Malcolm (*to* **Guy**)   I think I've come ... (*And exiting fast.*) Ursula!

He goes out leaving **Amelia** *and* **Guy** *alone. Pause.*

Guy   About last night – I'm terribly sorry, Milly ...

Amelia   You bastard!

Amelia *throws her glass of wine over* **Guy**, *turns and exits.*

Guy   Amelia!

Elizabeth *wanders in past* **Amelia**. *She takes her sunglasses off.*

Elizabeth   You haven't seen my father?

Guy *shakes his head.*

Elizabeth   Where the hell is he?

They both exit in opposite directions.

Scene Four

Tuesday morning. An office in north London. **Tony** *and* **Roger** *enter and unpack a new model computer while their boss* **Penny** *follows and looks on.* **Tony** *is very enthusiastic.*

Tony You see, Penny, my idea's that instead of getting canvassers battering our clients and any number of other businesses every three or four weeks with phone calls – which just piss them off anyway – we should set up a sort of database. We could have records at our fingertips – of what systems we've sold to them, any existing software and hardware they're using, and what they might require for the future – how they might expand. That way we could target our marketing more effectively – Roger and me, and the other reps would waste less time, and I'm willing to lay good money our estimate to sale conversion would be a hundred – two hundred per cent better . . .

Penny Yes, Tony – but what will it cost?

Tony Well, we can use the PCs and hardware we sell, and there're any number of people we deal with who'd design the software for us very cheaply – that's the easiest part. What you need to do is to get the telesales people doing some market research as well as pitching for sales appointments while they're on the phone. Get them trained up to work the new database, and put them in front of the computer terminals, which they've filled with the new detailed information we've got about our customers and potential buyers, and in two months from now, Penny, you'd be running the most efficient and productive computer sales operation in London. And with such an effective outfit we'll be ready to make the expansion into information technology which we're not exploiting as much as we could. God, Penny – we're selling businesses software solutions and we haven't even got one ourselves!

Pause. **Penny** *smiles.*

Well – what d'you think?

Penny   So – as well as paying for the design of the software, you'd want me to pay for the canvassers' training to use the system . . .

Tony   It'd be worth it in the long-term . . .

Penny   And how much lost business d'you think it'll cost me having the canvassers spend precious dialling time doing market research instead of pitching for appointments and sales?

Tony   It's an investment . . .

Penny   And how much d'you think those canvassers will want in extra wages as skilled computer operators? For God's sake, Tony – they'll all want contracts of employment! If I went to the MD with this hare-brained scheme I'd be laughed out of the office . . .

Tony   But, Penny . . .

Penny   No, Tony – Our phone operation's cheap enough – and the best way to keep the company running at a healthy profit is to maintain a stock of razor-sharp reps . . . (*A beat.*) I may as well tell you now, since we're on the subject, that you two'll have the opportunity to show your sales skills to me on Thursday afternoon . . .

Roger   What?

Penny   I'll be testing you both on your sales presentation technique so we can see what the real reason behind the dip in our figures might be, Roger. Now you two boys check that new baby there for damage – I'm just off for coffee.

Penny *turns and exits.*

Roger   I told you, Tony . . .

Tony   I can't believe she just dismissed it out of hand . . .

Roger   You know what it's like now, Tony – do it on the cheap, make a profit. They won't take the edge off a bonus, or a salary, to invest . . .

Tony   You have to invest – it's business sense . . .

Roger   It's a changed world now . . .

Tony   Yes – but you still have to invest in people – in technology – that's what I did with the factory –

Roger   And you still went under with everyone else. Accept it Tony – you were a King Canute in a changing world –

Tony   I believe in the free market for God's sake – I don't want to go back to the days when Jack Jones was running the country from the bloody TUC!

Roger   Leave it, Tony . . .

Tony *smiles and so does* **Roger** *acknowledging the enormous rapport the two men have.*

Tony   I can honestly say, Roger, with the exception of my godson, Joseph, you are the only socialist in the world I like.

Roger *laughs.*

Tony   God – what are we doing here, Roger?

Roger   Getting by, Tony, getting by. (*A beat.*) How's the wedding going?

Tony'*s face drops and his mood changes immediately as he busies himself with the computer.*

Roger   Tony? Tony? Are you all right? Tony? Are you all right?

Tony   I'm just a bit worried . . .

Roger   Are Henry and Elizabeth all right?

Tony *nods.*

Roger   Well, what then?

Tony   Please don't mention this to anyone in the office but . . . I don't know if I'm going to have enough money to pay for it all . . .

Roger   What?

Tony   Well, I was going to get a loan . . .

Roger   But I thought you had money in the bank?

Tony (*shaking his head*)   Just a few hundred quid . . . I mean, it's ridiculous, no one'll lend me any money – I've been credit blacklisted Roger. All those years, earning all that money, and I'm blacklisted . . . Can you believe it? And they said even if I can get myself off the blacklist, it's unlikely I'll get a loan big enough to cover the cost of the wedding, without any collateral – I mean – a bloody sales rep's too much of a risk . . .

Roger   How much money d'you need?

Tony   Forty grand . . .

Roger   Christ, Tony . . .

Tony   I'm trying to call in one or two favours . . .

Roger   What about the in-laws, Henry's parents?

Tony   I can't ask . . .

Roger   Why?

Tony   I just can't!

Pause.

I'm sorry.

Roger   That's all right.

Pause.

I should be off. I'm seeing a doctor this afternoon.

Tony   What's the matter?

Roger (*smiling*)   No – He wants a PC for the surgery . . .

Pause.

Chin up, you fucking Tory bastard.

Tony smiles. **Penny** *enters unnoticed by the two men.*

Tony (*smiling*)   Go on, piss off then, you old socialist git! – Five to four you close him!

Roger *smiles, turns to exit, brushing past* **Penny**.

Penny Go, go, go, Roger . . .

Roger *exits.*

Penny Politics, eh, Tony? I don't know – you two are like clucking hens sometimes. (*A beat.*) I had an unusually political afternoon yesterday. I discovered Harriet Harman and I share a hairdresser. Now isn't that funny? Some of our hairs are probably sharing a roller at this very moment . . .

Tony *starts to repackage the computer.*

Penny Now isn't that baby sexy, Tony?

Tony I'm sure it'll sell very well, Penny . . .

Penny Are you all right, Tony?

Tony Yeah . . .

Penny Well, you should be with the bonus you've got coming this month. Your figures are very attractive – unlike some . . .

Tony The cash'll come in handy . . .

Penny How's the wedding going?

Tony Fine.

Penny (*angling*) Have you sent the invitations out yet?

Tony They go to print next Monday.

Penny Really? – How's Jacqui?

Tony Fine.

Penny Nice lady, Jacqui – I can see why you left Annie . . . (*A beat.*) God – it comes to something when seeing a new model PC's the sexiest moment you've had for weeks . . . (*A beat.*) I do hope I didn't upset you earlier, Tony – you do know I respect you enormously . . .

Tony I know, Penny . . .

Penny It just doesn't feel right discussing that sort of thing in front of Roger, it doesn't feel right discussing that sort of thing in the office. What would the MD think if he walked in

on that sort of discussion? – he'd think we were plotting . . .
Perhaps if we went out for dinner one evening you could take
me through your plans . . .

Tony (*picking up the computer*)   You're the boss, Penny.

A beat.

Penny (*smiling as* **Tony** *exits*)   Yes – I am.

Scene Five

Wednesday evening. **Joseph**'s *new flat in Camden.* **Joseph** *is*
Tony's *godson and he enters accompanied by* **Amelia**. *He is wearing
a pair of leather trousers and* **Amelia** *has a small crucifix on her lapel.*

Joseph   What d'you think then, Milly?

They both pause and take in the room.

Amelia   It's great.

Joseph   This room's going to be fantastic when it's
decorated. I'm definitely going to put a bookcase over there
– I'm fed up having all my books in boxes.

Amelia   When are you moving the rest of your stuff in?

Joseph   Next week hopefully . . .

Amelia   It's so generous of your parents.

Joseph   They can't wait to get rid of me.

Pause. **Joseph** *looks up at the ceiling.*

Amelia   Joe . . . I've got you a little something . . . A
moving-in present . . .

Amelia *takes a small wrapped parcel from her bag and hands it to*
Joseph, *who smiles and carefully unwraps it. The present is a book.*

Joseph   *Bleak House.*

Pause.

Amelia   The flat'll be brilliant when you've got all your
stuff in . . .

Joseph   Cheers, it's one of my favourites . . .

He kisses her on the cheek.

Amelia   You've read it already? – I didn't know . . .

Joseph   But I haven't got a copy – not my own copy.

Pause.

You're very good to me, Milly.

Amelia   You're good to me.

Joseph   You've been a good friend to me.

Amelia   You've listened to me too.

Amelia *looks at her feet.*

Joseph   Are you OK? Milly? Are you all right?

Amelia   Not really. (*A beat.*) It's just Guy . . .

Joseph   I knew it, I knew it – The way he spoke to you on Saturday was disgusting . . . (*A beat.*) He's so preoccupied with himself . . .

Amelia   You don't understand . . .

Pause.

It's just . . . Guy thinks Nicholas's going to sack him – But it's ridiculous, Joey . . . They're hardly going to get rid of him with the election coming up. (*A beat.*) Things were becoming difficult anyway, but now he's getting so paranoid and jumpy. Every word, anyone says, he picks over and analyses . . .

Joseph   Tony said he's doing a good job . . .

Amelia   He is – but Guy's making things much worse, of course. He spent all of Sunday afternoon at the barbecue revelling in some stupid rumour that Sir Toby's got a dicky heart . . .

Joseph   Really? – He's got a heart problem?

Amelia   Of course not . . .

Joseph *thinks over what she's been saying and smiles broadly.*

Joseph Well, you know what you should do?

Amelia What?

Joseph Join the Labour party.

Joseph *grins and sits on the floor.* **Amelia** *smiles weakly.*

Amelia We're always talking politics, Joe . . .

Joseph Well, I can tell you – I'm just about pissed off with it myself, Milly . . . I've been thinking more and more about getting out of the country.

Amelia Really?

Joseph I don't know – travelling for a bit maybe. India, the Far East, Hong Kong . . .

Amelia Well, I don't think you'll find your New Jerusalem out there . . . (**Joseph** *smiles.*) Nicholas loves it out there, his wife Christine's out there at the moment . . .

Joseph Silly old buffer he is . . .

Amelia Well, you didn't mind taking your theatre ticket off him . . .

Pause. **Joseph** *stands up.*

It's not just Guy, it's something else, Joe.

Joseph What?

A beat.

Amelia For a long time now – well, since I first moved down here, there's been someone else . . .

Joseph You've been seeing someone else?

Amelia No – not at all. I've not been unfaithful to Guy. (*A beat. She half-smiles.*) Well, there was conference in Blackpool last November . . .

Joseph *grins.*

Amelia Seriously, Joe . . . There's been someone else who I've really liked, who I've got to meet and . . .

Joseph And you can't get that person out of your head?

Amelia   Yes.

Pause.

Joseph   I know exactly how you're feeling . . .

Amelia   You do?

Joseph   I'm feeling exactly the same . . .

Amelia   You are?

Pause.

Joseph   I've felt exactly the same about someone for a long time as well . . .

Pause.

Someone I know really well, Milly – a friend. I guess – you know – more like brother and sister . . .

Amelia   I know exactly what you mean . . .

Joseph   You do?

Amelia   Tell me . . .

Joseph   I can't . . .

Amelia   Tell me, Joseph . . .

Joseph   It's so difficult . . .

Amelia   You can say it – I've started to say . . .

Joseph   I can't . . .

Amelia   I promise – I promise it'll be a secret between me and you – our secret – I won't tell a soul . . .

Pause.

Joseph   I'm totally –

Amelia   Go on . . .

Joseph   I'm totally in love with Elizabeth . . . Oh Christ, I've said it . . . I've said it . . . I don't believe it, I don't believe . . . Oh God . . . What am I doing? What am I doing? I've known her all my life – and she's getting married to someone else in four months!

Pause.

What do you think of me? – You must think I'm a complete bastard – you're going to be a bridesmaid for God's sake.

Pause.

Amelia   It is a bit unexpected.

Pause.

Joseph   Oh thank you, Milly, thanks for listening . . . You won't say – will you, Milly?

Amelia   No.

She pauses, collects her thoughts and continues.

You just have to accept that she's getting married to Henry. You just have to accept that that was the decision she made . . .

Joseph   Yeah . . .

Amelia (*beginning to smile again at this*)   You have to make a decision about how you're going to move on – from this point . . .

Joseph   Yeah, you're right . . .

Amelia   You have to be positive, and you have to think – How can I direct my energy at dealing with this?

Joseph *flashes* **Amelia** *a smile of such warmth and genuine feeling, she can only respond in like.*

Joseph   You're right. You're so right, Amelia . . .

Amelia   I am right . . .

Joseph   Yes you are . . .

Amelia   It doesn't take much – I'm your friend – I pray for you, Joey. All you have to do is say . . .

They are interrupted by a doorbell ringing and freeze, surprised.

Joseph   I better answer that. Oh shit . . .

He exits quickly. **Amelia** *lets out a deep sigh and reaches into her bag for her cigarettes. She lights one up and picks up the copy of* Bleak

House. **Joseph** *comes back in with* **Tony** *who has a carrier bag containing four cans of lager.*

Joseph Well, tell Henry thanks for the thought, but I don't know why you brought them round. You know I don't drink . . .

Tony I thought this was supposed to be a bit of a flat-warming . . .

Joseph Not really – I just thought you'd want to see it . . .

Tony Hello, Milly – are you all right? – You look a bit white . . .

Joseph Milly, d'you have to smoke?

Amelia Just this one . . .

Tony Well, d'you mind if I have one?

Joseph You don't smoke . . .

Tony A beer, Joey, I've just sold three grands worth of gear – nice bonus that'll be . . .

Joseph Help yourself.

Pause as **Tony** *opens a can and begins to take a swig.*

Annie and Lizzie might be dropping in to have a look tonight as well . . .

Tony *coughs and splutters over his mouthful of beer.*

Tony Shit!

Joseph There's a problem?

Tony I just don't want to see them.

Joseph's *doorbell rings.*

Joseph That'll be them.

Tony I'm not here, I'm not here, right . . .

Joseph Tony . . .

Joseph *is interrupted by the doorbell ringing again.* **Tony** *gives* **Amelia** *his can of beer.*

Tony   Look, please, this really is very important. Trust me, Joey. I'll explain later – I just don't . . . (*A beat.*) I'm not here, right – Joey, Milly?

Joseph   Where are you?

Tony   In the bog . . . Trust me, Joseph!

Tony *exits.* **Joseph** *and* **Amelia** *exchange a bewildered look. The doorbell rings again.*

Joseph (*exasperated*)   All right, I'm coming . . .

Joseph *exits.* **Amelia** *takes a swig from the can and stubs her cigarette out on the floor. She realises what she has done, bends over and tries to rub the burn mark out, can't, so she stuffs the butt in a bag and puts the copy of* Bleak House *on top of the burn.* **Joseph**, **Annie** *and* **Elizabeth** *enter.*

Elizabeth   I don't know how you can wear those trousers in this heat . . .

Annie   Funny thing to be wearing trousers like that anyway . . .

Joseph   I was just about to go out, but I'll show you the living-room and the bedroom . . .

All three stop in their tracks immediately detecting something is afoot. **Joseph** *immediately assumes whatever has happened in his absence is connected with* **Tony**'s *subterfuge. Pause.* **Joseph** *plays it cool.*

Joseph   Is . . . er . . . the plumber still in the bathroom?

Amelia   The plumber?

Joseph   Yeah – the plumber – in the bathroom.

Amelia   Who?

Elizabeth   How many have you had, Amelia?

Amelia   Yes! He's still in there – the leak's really bad – terrible. In fact he said he's going to be at least another half an hour . . .

Annie   Well, could you just ask him, or her – well you never know these days, do you?

Joseph   No ...

Annie   Could you just ask if he could come out of there for a minute so I can use the lavatory?

Joseph   No.

Elizabeth   No?

Annie   I'm sure he won't mind. I'm bursting, Joe ...

Amelia   It's the water – he had to switch off the water while he's fixing the pipe.

Annie   Oh ...

Elizabeth   Well, look – we'll just have a quick nose at the bedroom, and we'll go, Mum. We can come back again at the weekend ...

Annie   All right then. Is that all right, Joe, only I'm bursting ...

Joseph   Yes. The bedroom's this way ...

They move towards the exit.

Annie   And I'll just have a quick peek at the bathroom ...

Joseph (*barring their way*)   No!

Elizabeth   Joseph, what the hell's the matter with you?

Amelia (*over-helpful*)   There's something in the bedroom ... That Joseph and I might not want you to see ...

Joseph   What?

Amelia   Remember?

Elizabeth   Is there, Joseph?

Pause.

Joseph   Yes ... Well ... No –

Elizabeth   What are you hiding?

Joseph }
Amelia }   Nothing ...

Pause.

Annie   You haven't got a contraption in there have you?

Pause.

Amelia (*checking her watch*)   Joseph ... Aren't we meant to be at the restaurant now?

Joseph   Yes ...

Elizabeth (*menacing and disbelieving*)   You're going out for dinner?

Joseph   Curry ...

Annie (*winking to* **Elizabeth**)   Well, you should have said, Joseph. We wouldn't have imposed if you'd told us you'd made other plans this evening. (*A beat.*) Come on, Elizabeth – I'm going to have an accident in a minute. See you then, Joe, Milly ...

Annie *and* **Elizabeth** *exit.* **Joseph** *and* **Amelia** *stand still, unmoved.*

Joseph   Oh fuck.

Amelia   Shit.

Joseph   Bollocks.

Amelia   I'm sorry – I was just trying to help – She seemed determined –

Elizabeth *steps back into the room.*

Elizabeth   By the way, Joseph, if you see my dad tell him to ring me.

Joseph *nods.* **Elizabeth** *smiles.*

Elizabeth   I don't know why you've been causing such a fuss – I'm pleased for you ... Christ – I never would have believed it – You two ...

Elizabeth *exits.* **Joseph** *and* **Amelia** *look at each other.* **Amelia** *smiles.* **Joseph** *is horrified. Pause.* **Tony** *wanders back in having taken in the room to check* **Elizabeth** *and* **Annie** *have gone.*

Tony   Lovely tiles you've got in the bathroom there, Joseph ... Shame all you had to read was a *Guardian*.

Pause.

Joseph   Hold on a minute, Tony. I don't know why but . . .

Tony's *mobile phone rings which he quickly digs out.*

Tony   Hello? Hello . . . Richard . . . How are you?

Pause.

I'm OK basically . . .

Pause.

Yeah – she's fine . . . Yes Jacqui's fine too . . .

Pause.

The wedding? Oh . . . OK . . .

Pause.

Yes, yes, should be a marvellous day . . . Yes, there was something I'd like to discuss with you . . .

Pause. He smiles.

What's tomorrow? Yes . . . Thursday . . . We should have lunch – Brilliant . . .

Pause.

See you then . . .

He switches off the phone and smiles, but notices **Joseph**'s *pissed off.*

I'm sorry, Joseph, I'm really very sorry – I just couldn't see them now.

Joseph   Yeah?

Tony   I'm sorry . . . (*A beat.*) I really should shoot off, Joey.

Pause.

Joseph – I'm sorry. (*A beat.*) I wasn't here, Joseph, OK? Amelia?

Joseph   I don't believe this . . .

Tony   I'm going to go. I'm going to go right now, Joey . . . See you, Amelia – I am sorry.

Amelia   It's all right. I'll see you, Tony.

Tony   See you then, Joey.

Joseph *doesn't answer.* **Tony** *exits.* **Joseph** *puts his head in his hands, wanders over to* **Amelia***, bends over, then crouches down onto his knees, takes the copy of* Bleak House *which he uses to strike himself on the forehead three times.*

Amelia   Come on, Joseph ... It's not that bad ... (*A beat.*) You know what Annie's like, she'll have forgotten all about it tomorrow morning and Tony – Tony wouldn't have wanted us to hide him if there wasn't a very good reason ... Joe? Joseph? What about a restaurant? – What about a curry? I'll buy you dinner, it's the least I can do ...

Joseph   What's that mark?

Amelia   What mark?

Joseph   The fucking mark on the floor ...

Amelia   Where?

Joseph   The fucking fag burn on the floor!

Pause. **Joseph** *slowly looks up at* **Amelia***.* **Amelia** *bursts into tears.*

Act Two

Scene One

Thursday afternoon. An office in north London. **Roger** *has a couple of folders, at hand.* **Penny** *stands by an easy-wipe upright board, studying intently, and flicking backwards and forwards pages of her notepad, ticking some remarks and crossing out other notes. On the board someone has written:* 'Product', 'Features', 'Quality', 'Cost', *and* 'Service Guarantee'. **Tony** *has a folder under his arm and looks at his feet. There is a long pause while* **Penny** *reviews her notes.*

Roger Well?

Penny *sighs and folds up her pad.*

Penny In one word, Roger – Amateurish.

Roger It wasn't that bad . . .

Penny I'm afraid it was. I now understand why you failed to get Dr Sarangwala for us on Tuesday and why when Tony went after him yesterday he closed the deal.

Pause.

Tony It was just luck . . .

Penny No such thing at all. (*Referring to her pad.*) Your presentation lasted – yes, here we are – twelve minutes exactly. Tell me, Roger, I'm intrigued, what did you hope to achieve in twelve minutes?

Pause.

Roger Well, I got through all the basics . . .

Penny The basics? You're not trying to sell a C5, Roger! – Jesus, Roger! Did you tell me about our reputation as a company, our client list? No. Did you tell me about our after-installation service, quality control and guarantee? You said you thought we were, I quote, 'not a bad firm for that sort of thing'. You're not actually a second-hand electrical goods salesman, Roger. Although, I have to say, that's what it sounded like to me. There was no detailed knowledge of our products. No mention of the processors – all ours are pentium processors – the system speed, or memory function. It did actually cross my mind that you didn't know anything at all about memory functions. (*She laughs.*) Do you actually know what RAM means?

Pause.

Tony   Random . . .

Penny   I know you know what it means, Tony.

Pause.

This is very disappointing, Roger. I had hoped these sales quality tests would be uniformly bright. Now I know why you have such an appalling turnover. Now why should I cover your arse when my boss looks at your figures and wants an explanation, Roger? Give me one good reason why I should spend an hour defending you as a valuable and viable asset to my team, when you could only give me twelve minutes of half-baked bullshit!

Pause.

Roger   I'm sorry. I'll turn myself around, Penny, it's just . . .

Penny   You better. Do you know how much you cost me in basic and expenses? I hope that you're more cost effective next month, for your sake and mine. (*A beat.*) I'm going for coffee.

Penny *folds up the easy-wipe board which she's going to take out with her.*

Roger   I'm sorry, Penny . . .

Penny   I'll be back in ten – so while I'm gone I suggest you take a good hard look at yourself and the shabby work I've had to sit through this afternoon. Sorry you've had to listen to this, Tony.

Penny *turns and exits.* **Tony** *grins and so does* **Roger** *– very schoolboyish. Pause.*

Roger   You did all right?

Tony   I wasn't much better – What happened with the doctor? When I saw him I closed him in half an hour ...

Roger   Well – the computer they had already was all right ... It didn't feel a very moral thing to be doing.

Pause. He smiles.

I don't think I'm cut out for sales ... (*A beat.*) God, I don't want to be here. I've got to get out, Tony –

Tony   You'll find something else ...

Roger   It's all right for you – you can talk to them.

He takes in a deep breath and sighs. Pause.

How's the wedding going?

Tony (*very serious*)   Terrible ...

Roger   I thought you were calling in some favours?

Tony (*shaking his head*)   I saw a guy I used to do business with for lunch today. Richard – my friend – he was so embarrassed. He thought I meant fifteen hundred, not fifteen grand. Nearly had a hernia when I said the figure on his cheque was wrong ...

Roger   It's a lot of money.

Tony   He said he'd lend me three, which I took, but there was no way he'd lend me that much without any sort of guarantee ...

Roger   What about Annie?

Tony   No – she's only got a couple of thousand kicking around and Guy told me she's looking for a job.

Roger   Why don't you just come clean? Speak to Henry's father –

Tony   I would do, I really would. It's just that not only is he bloody well paying for the honeymoon – but now he's setting them up in a restaurant. I've got to try and get the money, Roger. I've got to.

Roger   Come on, Tony. It doesn't have to be such a posh bash . . .

Tony   It's too late – everthing's booked . . .

Roger   Come clean . . .

Tony   There are one or two antique things in the flat I can try and shift . . . There's one picture which I'm sure I can get a few thousand for . . .

Roger   This is mad, Tony. This is absolutely crazy. You can't go on . . .

Tony   What? – I want the best for my daughter.

Roger   And you'd sacrifice everything for that?

Pause.

Look – for five, six, seven thousand even . . . You can have a perfectly good – a very good – wedding for that sort of money . . .

Tony   It's not what I want . . .

Roger   It's unreal, Tony, and you and your daughter are kidding yourselves if you don't realise how far out of touch this wedding's got . . .

Tony   No it's not . . .

Roger   Come on, Tony. From the minute I started work here I've heard every detail. The hotel, designer dress, the people that are coming. It's grotesque . . .

Tony   Roger . . .

Roger   Don't you realise that this sort of thing ended the minute your business went to the wall . . .

Tony   I haven't struggled all my life . . .

Roger   You're not the only one . . .

Tony   I didn't build myself up so at the end of it all I can't even pay for my daughter . . . For my only daughter to have a wedding on the cheap . . .

Roger   But she's not going to get a wedding on the cheap for that sort of money! How much do you think people spend on weddings?

Tony   I don't care – you're supposed to be my mate . . .

Roger   I am – which is why I'm trying to get some sense into you.

Pause.

People like us – we all did all right a few years back . . .

Tony   What do you mean, people like us?

Roger   We had careers, we all made a few quid. I've got daughters – don't you think I'd like to give them forty grand weddings?

Tony   Leave off, Roger . . .

Roger   You had a taste of the good life. You've had a taste of class . . .

Tony   Shut up . . .

Roger   Nothing like a good English wedding for class snobbery . . .

Tony   Shut up, will you . . .

Roger   Join the bloody Tory party and you think . . .

Tony   Why don't you just give your socialist bollocks a rest!

Pause.

I don't need this . . .

Roger   Have you ever asked me?

Tony   What?

Roger   About my politics?

Tony   Piss off . . .

Roger   Have you ever asked me if I'm a socialist?

Tony   What are you getting at?

Roger   You've never actually asked me . . .

Tony   Well, what are you then?

Roger   You've never asked me about what I used to do . . .

Tony   Well, what then?

Roger   You've never asked me what I used to do, about my wife and my kids. In fact you've never actually asked me if I'm married.

Tony   So?

Roger   You've always assumed, or just ignored me, wrapped up in your own fucking arrogant world . . .

Tony   What is this here!

Roger   And you treat what I say with such indifference . . .

Tony   Roger!

Roger   Like I'm a second-class citizen, you label me a 'socialist' – attach it like it's a fucking dirty word! I've been a Tory voter all my life, I went to Oxford University, I was a civil servant, I used to have a big house – but that wouldn't make a difference to your sneering inflated fucking arrogance even if you knew it. They used to say don't ask a public schoolboy about his education because he'll bore your pants off. Now, it's better not to ask a self-made idiot from the last ten years how he made and lost his first fortune because he'll tell you blow by blow how he crawled up out of the gutter, trampled over everyone he ever knew to make a fast buck and get the Merc, only to blow it all – and expect me! – expect me to feel sorry for him! It's people like you that have torn this country apart, with your fucking arrogance, your gutter newspapers, and your fucking obsession with everything you envied from your stupid slums!

Tony   How dare you!

Roger   People like you have torn my life apart! – And you expect me to feel sorry because you can't have a wedding for forty thousand pounds! How dare you!

Long pause. They are both shocked by the ferocity of **Roger**'s *anger.*

People like me –

Tony   Leave it!

Roger   People like me don't expect anything any more . . .
Fine, I always had a head start over the man in the street . . .
Just as long as people like you don't tell me how hard life is for
them now . . .

Tony   Enough, Roger!

Roger   I don't want to know about your house prices . . .

Tony   Roger!

Roger   And I don't want to know about your hard-luck
stories about your wedding . . .

Tony   I don't want to hear any more!

Pause. **Penny** *enters. She has a mug of coffee in her hands.*

Penny   All right boys?

Pause.

Roger, could you go through to my office. I'd like to speak to
you about your performance this afternoon alone if you don't
mind. I'll be through after I've chatted to Tony – so let's
hope you've picked up one or two tips from him.

Roger *glances at* **Tony** *and exits.*

Penny   D'you know what I'd like, Tony?

Tony (*hard*)   I've got no idea, Penny.

Penny   I'd like you to go over to the door and lock it, and
pull down the blinds, and then I'd like you to come over here
and put your hand on the inside of my leg – and then touch
me . . .

Pause. She smiles.

Just joking – just a joke. You know you shouldn't be so
uptight with me, Tony. I like you. You're a good rep. You're
a valuable asset to me and you're a good worker. You look
after me, Tony, you keep me in the position I'm in. I look
after the people who look after me . . .

Tony   What is this, Penny?

Penny   You always get the choice of the leads, Tony ...

Tony   I haven't asked for special treatment ...

Penny   I know, Tony – that's why I like you. You're modest. I like modesty – it's something I'm not. (*A beat.*) I want you to do something for me, Tony. I'd like you to go back through Roger's leads and clients and check out the blow-outs ...

Tony   But, Penny ...

Penny   Come on, Tony, on the basis of this afternoon and the doctor, how much other business do you think Roger's just let go?

Tony   He's my friend ...

Penny   You know as well as I do he's on the way out and any loose ends, any business it's yours ...

Tony   I can't ...

Penny   Of course you can – and don't tell me you don't need the money –

Tony   And what's that supposed to mean?

Penny   Well, I heard the wedding's costing you about fifty grand. I'm sorry but I don't know anyone in this job if they've got that sort of cash kicking around ...

Tony   That's none of your business ...

Penny   But it makes business sense, right, Tony? Come on, I've heard you talk about the factory, I've heard you talk about us here. Cost efficiency and personal motivation go hand in hand, you've said it as much as me. Roger's finished, whatever you decide.

Pause.

Tony   I need to think about it. (*A beat.*) He's my friend, Penny, he's a person, he's a human being ...

Penny   Oh, come on, Tony, what the hell do you care about Roger . . . You were quick enough to run after Dr Sarangwala . . . (*A beat.*) Look I'm tired of this. You know how it is, Tony, you scratch my back, and I'll scratch yours. It's a lot harder out there without me pushing things your way . . .

Tony   What the fuck are you saying?

Penny   Don't be such a bully now, Tony. I've given you a chance so you just have to get your finger out of your arse and get on with it . . .

Tony   What is this?

Penny   I'd hate to see you become another statistic – eh, Tony? I can make things work for you . . . (*A beat.*) Anyway, why don't you get on the phone and check out some other doctors – I'm sure they're all upgrading these days . . . More business, Roger's leads and you'll be my superstar, Tony. You play your cards right and I'll let you buy me dinner. I'd like that – wouldn't you?

Scene Two

Friday evening. **Henry** *and* **Elizabeth**'s *house in north London.* **Joseph** *and* **Annie** *follow* **Henry** *into the dining-room.*

Henry   This is the dining-room, Joseph . . .

Annie   I can't believe you haven't been here before.

Joseph   I know.

Annie   It's a nice house, isn't it?

Joseph   Yeah . . . it's great.

Annie   Lizzie and Henry are buying a new dining-table to put in here, aren't you, Henry?

Henry   Yes . . .

Annie   Henry, why on earth are you wearing that jacket in this unbearable heat?

Henry (*grinning*)   You'll have to excuse me – Got to push on in the kitchen . . .

Annie *nods and* **Henry** *exits.*

Annie   I think they want something to seat eight . . .

Joseph   Expecting lots of people over?

Annie   They're very good at that sort of thing.

Joseph   It's the sort of thing you're born into, isn't it?

Annie   I suppose so.

Joseph   Knowing which knife and fork to pick up. When to eat the mints.

Annie *smiles.*

Joseph   I went to an NUS conference a couple of years ago. They had a sort of dinner at the end, and one of the reps – this guy from Wigan – started chewing the mints before they brought in the starter. Someone noticed and he was absolutely taken apart, by everyone. I mean – he didn't know any different, did he? – and there are a bunch of right-on middle-class prats, ripping him apart.

Annie   Your conscience, Joey – you are sweet . . . (*A beat.*) You know, I was a liberal when I was your age . . .

Pause. **Joseph** *shakes his head.*

Joseph   Don't talk to me like my politics is a fad . . .

Annie   I didn't mean it like that.

Joseph   I didn't ask to be born into a rich family.

Pause.

Annie   I didn't realise you were so friendly with Amelia?

Joseph   About Wednesday . . .

Annie   Honestly, Joey, I'm not making any judgements . . .

Joseph   I'm really not up to anything funny . . .

Annie I know you're not. I just think you should realise that Amelia and Guy may be going through a bad patch – I don't want you to get hurt, that's all . . .

Joseph There's nothing going on between me and Amelia.

Annie If you say so.

Joseph In fact – there's someone else.

Annie I didn't know you had a girlfriend, Joe?

Henry *wanders in and stops still. He's taken his jacket off, wears an apron, is sucking his left thumb and has half a cucumber in his right hand, which he lifts, as if it will explain his presence. He wanders out of the other exit. Pause.*

Joseph What is it Lizzie likes about Henry?

Annie What d'you mean? He's incredibly nice – he treats Elizabeth very well – a real gent.

Joseph I never thought Liz would marry a city toff . . .

Annie He's not like that. That's just how you see him. You're actually quite similar . . .

Joseph No . . .

Annie You're both kind, and passionate about things . . .

Joseph Henry? Passionate? What's Henry ever got worked up about?

Annie He's an excellent cook . . .

Joseph *laughs.*

Annie You try and get in the kitchen while he's cooking – he'll chase you out with a frying-pan . . .

Joseph Yeah, right. Like food's something really important?

Annie It is to Henry.

Joseph But he doesn't believe in anything, does he?

Annie Does that matter?

Joseph Of course it does . . .

Annie   Not everyone has to fight causes . . .

Henry *re-enters. He shows off a plaster on his left thumb.*

Henry   That's better – cut it doing the bloody salad. You OK there, Joe? Sorry I can't come and chat but I've got to get the dinner ready. Wouldn't you like to go into the sitting-room?

Annie   We're talking, Henry.

Henry   Right-ho . . .

Annie   Thank God you've taken that jacket off . . .

Henry   Got to take it off while I'm cooking – it's the only time you'll see me without a jacket on. Daddy's always said you can tell the mark of a gentleman by the cut of his jacket. It's my uniform I suppose – I didn't take to the army and chaps like me don't go for the church these days – so I've got my pinstripe and casuals . . .

Pause.

Still, it'll all change when we've got the restaurant, eh, Annie? – I'll be cooking all the time . . . D'you like peppers in your salad, Joe?

Joseph *nods and* **Henry** *smiles and exits.*

Joseph   You're right – Henry doesn't have to fight a cause . . . The rich have always been able to sit back, make a pile and rule the bloody country. Forty-five made things better for a lot of people . . .

Annie   What do you know about forty-five?

Joseph   People like Nicholas – people who run things don't get into trouble . . .

Annie   Not always.

Joseph   Look at Tony . . . the poor bastard's out there breaking his back, travelling all over the country hawking bloody computers he can't understand. D'you really think he can use a computer?

Annie *laughs.*

Joseph   Sell them, maybe. Work one? No way.

Annie   Have you seen him?

Pause.

Is he all right?

Joseph   I think things aren't too good with Jacqui . . .

Annie   I knew it! I knew it wouldn't last – Frankly, I'm surprised it's lasted this long . . .

Joseph   I don't think they're splitting up . . .

Pause.

Annie   Aren't you surprised it lasted this long? The way she bosses him around, she's just a mouthy little bitch . . .

Joseph   Jacqui's all right . . .

Annie   What! You like her?

Joseph   She's a nice lady . . .

Annie   But not that nice that she didn't commit adultery with my husband. D'you know how I felt, Joey?

Joseph   I know . . .

Annie   I felt betrayed, used – totally useless, Joseph. I couldn't compete . . .

Pause.

What's it going to be like at the wedding? How d'you think having her there's going to make me feel? You know sometimes over the last six years I've wanted to scream the house down with the pain she's caused. But it's not all about making an issue out of things – fighting causes, Joey. You've just got to cope, get by, and stand by the people you love most.

Pause.

I'm surprised at you, Joey – I'm very surprised that she's managed to suck you in as well . . .

Joseph   I'm sorry . . .

Annie   She's a parasite.

Elizabeth *enters. She has bags full of shopping.*

Elizabeth   Look what I've done with Henry's credit card . . .

Annie   What have you got?

Elizabeth   Everything . . . Just a sec, Mum – I need to use the loo . . . (*On her way out.*) Hello, Joey . . .

Joseph   All right . . .

Elizabeth *exits.*

Joseph   Actually I've been thinking about leaving the country . . .

Annie   What?

Joseph   You know, travelling – finding somewhere else to live – Australia maybe. See the Far East then – I don't know what . . .

Annie   I never knew you wanted to do anything like that . . .

Joseph   I need a change.

Pause.

Politics has been my life for the past seven years – I cried when we lost in ninety-two, and I cried when John Smith died. And now when we're nearly there, we're nearly there, I don't know if we're going to change a damn thing, and those self-interested bastards in the City are going to have it their way . . .

Annie   They're not all like that –

Joseph   No?

Annie   Henry's not like that . . .

Joseph   We'll get turfed out after five years and that's it until you lot need another kick up the arse . . .

Annie   Let's leave this, Joey . . .

Joseph   I want us to change things – really change things. I don't want the country to smile on Tony Blair in the last week of the election and then spend five years realising it's all been a load of soundbites . . . I don't know – Jesus – Perhaps you lot are meant to rule . . .

Annie   It's just Britain . . .

Joseph   Capitalism . . .

Annie   I think you'll find it's class . . .

Henry *enters, tea-towel in hand.*

Henry   Class? I'll tell you one thing – this meal's bloody class . . .

Elizabeth *enters, half a cucumber in hand.*

Elizabeth   Henry – explain . . .

Henry   I wondered where that went . . .

Elizabeth   Why am I marrying you? Don't hang about in here, Mum – Let's go through.

Joseph   I like this room.

Elizabeth   It's not bad . . .

Henry   Did you get my pinstripe from the cleaners?

Elizabeth   Yes, it's in the car . . .

Annie   That suit's been through the wars, eh, Henry?

Elizabeth   Milly got wine all over it . . .

Henry   The hooligan with the Toblerone got ash all over it . . .

Annie   Malcolm was sick on it . . .

Joseph   Malcolm?

Henry   At the engagement party – He got carted on a bottle of gin and threw up on my shoulder . . .

Annie   Wear an anorak for the stag night . . .

Henry   I'm wearing my wellies for that! Got all sorts of people from Rugby coming down for it . . .

Joseph   Didn't you spill something on it when you proposed?

Henry   Asparagus soup . . .

Annie   How did you manage that?

Henry   I tucked the table cloth in my trousers by mistake and when I got onto my knee . . .

Elizabeth   The candles went over as well and burnt a hole in my dress . . .

Annie   You are accident prone . . .

Henry   Yeah . . . (*Shouting.*) Watch out!

Joseph, **Annie** *and* **Elizabeth** *duck. Pause.*

Henry   Just kidding . . . (*He laughs.*)

Elizabeth   Henry! Get into the kitchen and get the dinner – and take this . . . (*Passes the cucumber.*)

Henry *exits.*

Annie   He's marvellous – You've made the right choice, Lizzie . . .

Elizabeth   I know . . .

Annie   I love a wedding . . . It's so . . . English – English as cricket and poppies my sister always says. The hymns and that gorgeous church you're having – and Henry's wonderful . . .

Elizabeth   And such a whizz in the kitchen . . . The restaurant's going to be fab . . .

Annie   Well, he loves food . . .

Elizabeth   You know the first time Henry cooked for me – he said the sweetest thing. He said that he liked nothing more than to cook for me, because – for him, making someone a meal's his way of showing he cares – his love . . .

Annie   That's right ...

Elizabeth   You only have to look at it on the plate – it's arranged so carefully ...

Annie   You'll be a success – I know you will.

Elizabeth   Are you all right, Joe?

Joseph   Just thinking ... About coming over here ...

Elizabeth   To talk to us?

Joseph   Yeah. I wanted to tell you in person ...

Annie   What's this, Joey?

Elizabeth   I'll call Henry in ... Henry! Henry!

Joseph   It's all right ...

Annie   No – go on, Joseph ...

Henry *enters wiping his hands on a tea-towel.*

Elizabeth   Joseph's got something to tell us ...

Joseph   It's something I've been thinking about for a while ...

Pause.

Elizabeth   Well? – What is it?

Scene Three

Saturday morning. The hard shoulder of the M11 Northbound between Theydon Bois and Harlow. The roar of passing traffic. **Tony** *stands quite directly in front of the audience.* **Jacqui** *runs on.*

Jacqui   What the fuck are you doing stopping the car like that!

Tony   Leave me alone!

Jacqui   We could've been killed ...

Tony   I should be so lucky ...

Jacqui   Well, fine! Go on – why don't you just do it! Stop talking about it, like you talk about everything and just go right ahead and walk into the road – Go on – it's right in front of you . . .

Tony   Leave me alone!

Jacqui   Go on – you can find a car. I should think it'll be easier to throw yourself under a car than it's going to be explaining to your bloody daughter!

Tony   Well, thanks – thanks for that support . . .

Jacqui   Support? Jesus, Tony . . . You stay out all night, roll in at nine o'clock this morning and you practically drag me out into the car . . . You drive like a madman, and now you suddenly cut across the dual carriageway and run out of the car like a lunatic! What the hell is this, Tony!

Pause.

Tony   I've fucked things up . . .

Jacqui   You've noticed then?

Tony   No – I've really screwed things up . . .

Jacqui   What? What's happened?

Pause.

What happened last night? Tell me . . .

Pause.

Tony   Yesterday morning while you were out . . .

Jacqui   Go on . . .

Tony   I took the landscape down . . .

Jacqui   My grandmother's painting?

Tony   An old friend of mine . . . He deals in antiques – He couldn't lend me any money – but I mentioned the painting . . .

Jacqui   That was passed on to me when my father died!

Tony   He said he'd do me a favour and give me two thousand for it . . .

Jacqui   I don't believe this . . .

Tony   So I sold it to him . . .

Jacqui   My painting!

Tony   And I drove away . . . and I had the cash . . .

Jacqui   If you'd . . .

Tony   But I stopped the car. I felt like . . . A common criminal. And I thought – Is this what I've become? And I knew that when you came home, and saw the picture had gone, what would happen – You'd leave – The one thing that I have left . . .

Pause.

By the time I got back to Roy he'd already sold it on for four thousand –

Jacqui   I don't believe . . .

Tony   I had to near on throttle him to get him to tell me where the buyer was. (*A beat.*) He wanted five back. I gave him Roy's two in cash, and assured him Roy'd guarantee a cheque for the other three . . .

Pause.

I came home. I put the picture back up. And I got my last four hundred quid out of the cashpoint . . . And I went to the casino . . .

Jacqui   What?

Tony   I was three grand in front by five o'clock, but – you know how it is – you make a few quid, you lose a few quid . . .

Pause.

Jacqui   So what do you want me to say to you, Tony? You're right – if you'd sold that painting – I wouldn't be here now . . . But what the hell makes you think I want to stay with you anyway?

Tony Are you saying you're going to leave?

Jacqui I've thought about it ...

Tony Well, fine – why don't you just get in the car and piss off ...

Jacqui What is this crap?

Tony All I want now that things have got tough is a bit of support ...

Jacqui Support? Support, support, support! What d'you think I've been doing for the last seven years! What d'you think I was doing when you went bankrupt? What d'you think I've been doing every day of the week when you come home, and moan about the people you've seen, and the office, and the news and the fucking journey into London ...

Tony All right ...

Jacqui What the hell d'you think I've done for you but offer you support! Well, I'm fed up offering you support – and at least this bloody wedding has done one thing for me – It's made me realise how much you take me for granted ...

Tony Jacqui ...

Jacqui Don't you think I take the tube into work! Don't you think I get pissed off with things and want support sometimes?

Tony Jacqui –

Jacqui You're not going to take me for granted any more! If we're going to make this work ...

Tony What I've ...

Jacqui If we're going to continue to ...

Tony Jacqui –

Jacqui Then you've got to start talking to me and stop walking all over me.

Pause.

Tony   What I'm trying to say – What I'm trying to communicate – is that . . . Yesterday, despite everything – All I wanted in the world was to come home . . .

Pause.

I love you. (*A beat.*) When was the last time you told me you loved me?

Jacqui   It's not enough just to say it any more . . .

Tony   I'm trying to say something here . . .

Jacqui   It's not enough for me – words won't change a thing . . .

Tony   But it's a start . . .

Jacqui (*shaking her head*)   What proof have you got that things are going to be any different in six months time – six years time?

Tony   I promise you . . .

Jacqui   You've promised your daughter a forty-grand wedding, but she's not going to get it . . .

Tony   Jacqui!

Jacqui   I'm not going to become another precious Annie . . .

Tony   She's got nothing to do with this . . .

Jacqui   I'm not going to be left for the next one to come along and fall for your dreams . . .

Tony   I've changed . . .

Jacqui   I don't want to be another bloody loyal woman racking your conscience for the next ten years . . .

Pause.

Tony   You know, Jacqui – I don't know if I ever told you this, but when I was a boy, I used to watch my father making his match-stick ships at the table in our front room. He made these magnificent models, some of them modern, some of them great things with tall masts. (*A beat.*) I never knew why he did that . . . I never knew . . .

Pause.

He never said, he never uttered a word – and I mean – my mother never knew . . . I don't know what he was doing – but I know what it means to me . . . As far as I know my father had never been on a boat . . . It's a simple thing to want . . .

Jacqui   He might not have wanted that . . .

Tony   It's a simple ambition to have – a simple dream . . .

Jacqui   You have no proof . . .

Tony   I don't need any proof! I can see it in everyone I ever knew at home. That spark that says I want things. (*A beat.*) They've got it all right, Jacqui. People have that, but they're just afraid to say it because of their place. Well, you've got to fight that and you've got to make things happen . . .

Jacqui   But you're not making us happen . . .

Tony   Well, what do you want from me?

Jacqui   You know what I want . . .

Tony   No – No I don't.

A beat.

Jacqui   I want a commitment . . .

Tony   What sort of commitment?

Jacqui   I'm thirty-four, Tony . . .

Pause.

You know what I want – Come on, you can only leave so many magazines on the side . . .

Pause.

I want to come off the pill.

Pause.

Tony   But we're not married – I mean if . . .

Jacqui (*smiling*)   Are you asking?

Tony   No – Definitely not . . .

They both laugh. Pause.

You won't be working . . .

Jacqui   I'll be having a baby . . .

Tony (*shaking his head*)   We just can't . . .

Jacqui (*deadly serious*)   Don't you dare say it . . .

Tony   Jacqui . . .

Jacqui   You say that, you dare say that now, and I walk over to the car and drive, and you never see me again . . .

Tony   But I haven't got anything to give a baby . . .

Jacqui   You have yourself . . .

Tony   I'm a terrible example . . .

Jacqui   Don't make excuses . . .

Tony   I've just been at a casino all night . . .

Jacqui   I'm serious, Tony . . .

Tony   I was going to sell your grandmother's heirloom . . .

Jacqui   This is what I want, Tony . . .

Tony   I've got no confidence any more . . . I haven't got any friends, I don't have my family . . .

Jacqui   You've got me, you'll have the baby . . .

Tony   I don't feel that I control things any more . . .

Jacqui   You could be run over by a car tomorrow . . .

Tony   I used to walk into the office and I'd look out onto the factory floor and all the women would be packing all those sweets, all different colours . . .

Jacqui   It's gone now, Tony . . .

Tony   I felt so proud of what I had – and what I was making . . .

Jacqui It's history . . .

Tony I'll never forget that . . .

Jacqui Those days are gone . . .

Pause.

Tony When Elizabeth was little I used to take her round to the girls. They loved her, she was such a pretty little girl – and they didn't let her have too many sweets because of her teeth, and she always came out with her pockets full of bits of silver . . .

Pause.

Jacqui Is this it?

Pause.

Tony Come to the hotel with me, Jacqui.

Jacqui No . . .

Tony Just help me this time . . .

Jacqui No.

Tony Just help me get through it . . .

Jacqui No.

Tony Help me tell Elizabeth . . .

Jacqui You come home with me.

Tony But I was going to the hotel . . .

Jacqui Yes – you were going to the hotel . . .

Tony Once I've got this over it'll be a new start . . .

Jacqui No – you come home with me – or it's over.

Tony But I've got to tell her!

Pause.

Jacqui Fine.

Jacqui *turns and exits.*

Tony Jacqui!

He stands still, sighs, and looks up. There's a rumble of thunder.

Christ ...

Scene Four

Noon on Saturday. The ballroom of a hotel in Hertfordshire. **Guy** *follows* **Amelia** *in.* **Amelia** *wears a coat, and both of them are wet from the rain.*

Guy   Please, Amelia ...

Amelia   No, Guy, it's over ... (*A beat.*) Please, let's just leave this now ...

Long pause.

Look at this room. It's magnificent.

Guy *surveys the room.*

Guy   I came to a spring ball here in eighty-eight.

Amelia   Did you?

Guy   They were all here. Thatcher, Lawson, Howe ... I remember seeing Tebbit with his wife in a wheelchair, the poor cow ...

Amelia   It's an amazing place for the wedding. Elizabeth's so lucky ...

Pause.

Guy   I have to ask you this – Is it someone else?

Amelia   No.

Guy   Who is it?

Amelia   It's not anyone!

Elizabeth *and* **Ursula** *enter,* **Elizabeth** *shaking an umbrella.*

Elizabeth   Hello, Milly, Guy ...

Guy   All right ...

Ursula   You're in big trouble, Guy ...

Guy What?

Ursula Apparently Nicholas's been told that you started that rumour about Sir Toby's dicky ticker – He's furious . . .

Guy Was it Malcolm?

Elizabeth Ursula doesn't solicit information from Malcolm . . .

Ursula That's quite enough . . .

Elizabeth He gets an erection every time she speaks to him . . .

Ursula Malcolm can stick his over-excited prick up his arse . . .

Annie *enters wearing a raincoat and shaking an umbrella.*

Annie Hello, Lizzie, hello, everyone . . .

Elizabeth Hi, Mum . . .

Annie You're looking very well, Ursula . . .

Ursula Thanks . . .

Annie Super. Thank God it's rained, I was beginning to feel suffocated in all that heat . . .

Elizabeth I like the sun.

Annie Hello, Guy, Amelia – Has Lizzie told you why we asked you along, Guy?

Guy No – Not yet.

Elizabeth It's Joseph –

Amelia What?

Elizabeth Joseph came over to see us last night. He wanted to tell us he's going away . . .

Amelia He's definitely going?

Annie Yes.

Ursula Where?

Elizabeth   The Far East. Apparently he's wanted to go off and travel for ages . . .

Amelia   But the flat . . .

Annie   It's such a shame, such a lovely flat . . .

Ursula   Oh, you've seen it, haven't you?

Elizabeth   Anyway – we're in need of a chief usher . . .

Amelia   He's not coming back for the wedding?

Annie   He's going to be out there for the year . . .

Amelia   When's he leaving?

Elizabeth   He's booked a flight for tomorrow morning.

Amelia   What? – A Sunday?

Guy   Bloody hell – Are you sure he's all right? – Funny to just decide to leave like that.

Pause.

Elizabeth   Well – we thought – given that Milly's a bridesmaid it might be nice if we asked you to step in, Guy . . .

Amelia   Lizzie . . .

Guy   I'd be delighted.

Elizabeth *moves over to* **Annie** *and* **Ursula**.

Elizabeth   I'm so excited. Henry and I paid the balance for Bali this morning . . .

Annie   Great . . .

Elizabeth   It's just paradise . . .

Annie   I know. Have you spoken to your father?

Elizabeth   Yes, I just got him on his mobile – He's on his way.

Annie   Is he going to give you a cheque? – You know, to cover things?

Elizabeth   He said he'd talk to me about everything when he got here.

Annie   You know, this might sound foolish – but I did think for a while, that your father has been deliberately avoiding us . . .

Annie, **Elizabeth** *and* **Ursula** *laugh*.

It even crossed my mind that he couldn't afford to pay for the wedding . . .

They laugh even more.

And that was why he's been avoiding us!

They fall about laughing.

Ursula   You are silly . . .

Elizabeth   This really is the happiest I've been in a long time . . .

This sentiment even touches **Ursula**.

Annie   How are Henry's swimming lessons going?

Elizabeth   Fine. He did two widths yesterday without stopping.

Annie   Good – You can't go on a honeymoon to Bali with a husband in waterwings . . .

Elizabeth *winks at* **Annie**.

Elizabeth   You know, I've been reconsidering peach – for the bridesmaids . . .

Annie   Really, Lizzy?

Ursula   Peach?

Stony silence.

You know very well I can't abide peach.

Malcolm *enters, wearing Wellington boots and a green Barbour jacket.*

Malcolm   Hi, everyone. Hello, Annie . . . (*He embraces her.*) Ursula – You look stunning . . .

Ursula   Yes – blue does suit me rather . . .

Elizabeth   But peach – would suit – Don't you think, Malcolm?

Malcolm *knows something is afoot and hesitates.*

Malcolm   Well . . . I think you look great in both . . .

He turns to **Guy** *and* **Ursula** *puts her fingers in her mouth.*

I saw the old chap with the VC on Thursday, Guy . . . Turns out the bugger next door didn't have planning permission in the first place so we're going to slap a court order on him . . . The old boy was over the moon – even agreed to have his picture taken with me for the local rag. Nice piece of publicity for us, eh, Guy?

He turns back towards **Elizabeth**.

Where's Henry?

Nicholas *enters. He wears a bowler hat, sports a row of medals and has a brolly.*

Nicholas   Hellow, everyone. Hello, Annie. Hello, Lizzie . . . (*He embraces them in turn.*) Sorry I'm late – the service ran over . . .

Annie   How was it?

Nicholas   Very Masonic . . . Feeling better, Amelia? – Shame you missed the Shakespeare . . . Still, I've got some tickets for the opera next week care of some Yanks – There are some benefits of being high up in banking, you see. Ever seen a *Turandot* before, Lizzie?

Elizabeth   No . . .

Nicholas   I know they used 'Nessun Dorma' for the football but it still gets me . . . (*Notices* **Guy**.) Guy!

This silences everyone. **Nicholas** *holds back.*

We need to talk . . .

Guy   Fine – there's a pub over the road . . .

Nicholas   Not now – later . . . (*He turns back to* **Annie**.) How are you?

Annie   Fine ...

Elizabeth (*looking at her watch*)   I hope dad's not going to be late ...

Annie   I shouldn't think so ...

Nicholas   God knows where Henry is. He was meant to meet me at the station ... (*A beat.*) What exactly are we discussing now?

Elizabeth   Well, we thought it would be a good idea to have an initial meeting here at the hotel – for all the key players ... And we need to get a rough idea on numbers – so I can go to the printers ...

Nicholas   Shouldn't this wait till Christine gets back?

Elizabeth   This is booked out every Saturday from now ... Nearly everyone's here – Tony and Henry are on their way ...

Nicholas   Quite – But my wife's in Hong Kong.

Pause.

This is lovely, Lizzie – Must be costing Tony a bomb ...

Elizabeth   I like it.

Nicholas   Where are you putting the wedding list?

Elizabeth   We thought Harrods ...

Nicholas   Harrods?

Elizabeth   Probably the best place for it – given the mix of people coming – You know, my father's relatives ...

Ursula   Fifty green and gold ashtrays for you then, Lizzie ...

Nicholas   And where are these people coming from?

Elizabeth   Mostly from parts of east London. Some from Essex and one or two from Scotland ...

Nicholas   Ah, some Scots – perhaps we'll dance a reel, eh, Annie?

Elizabeth   We're getting a string quartet for the afternoon in here, and then they're moving into the bar, and a jazz band are coming for the evening . . .

Nicholas   Great.

Elizabeth   Paid the balance for Bali this morning . . . It's going to be heaven . . .

Nicholas   If you get Henry through customs. You know when he was a boy a toy pistol in his bag caused a major security alert at Heathrow. Thank God the Lifeguards didn't take to him. What the hell would he do with a real gun . . .

He smiles.

I can't wait for this wedding – And Sir Toby's going to speak. It'll be a real morale booster for the constituency . . .

Elizabeth   It's a wedding not a political rally, Nicky!

Nicholas   You really don't understand the Tory party, do you, my dear?

Annie *smiles.*

Nicholas   D'you want a cheque now?

Tony *enters – and briefly unnoticed – as* **Nicholas** *takes out his wallet. He is soaking wet.*

Nicholas   Hello there, Tony – you're drenched . . .

Elizabeth   Are you all right, Daddy?

Tony   I'm soaking wet.

Elizabeth   Why are you so wet?

Tony   It's raining. I just walked the last mile to get here.

Nicholas   You should've got a taxi.

Tony   I didn't have any change – What is this? – Twenty questions . . .

Annie   All right, Tony . . .

Tony   Hello, Ursula – Guy. Hello, Malc, Milly . . .

Turns to **Annie**.

Hello, Annie.

Pause. He moves closer to **Elizabeth**. **Annie** *is in earshot.*

Well, what's this all about then?

Elizabeth   A first meeting – for the key players ...

Tony   This isn't the Yalta summit ...

Elizabeth   There's a lot to organise. We're behind really – but you've been so difficult to get hold of ...

Tony   Yeah ...

Elizabeth   We've had to just go ahead and get on with some things ...

Tony   I thought what was meant to happen was that you talked things over with me first and then we decided what we can have and then have a meeting ...

Elizabeth   Well, I've tried to ... I've been ringing you all week but your phone's always switched off ...

Pause.

I saw a sample invitation this morning ... It was beautiful – engraved in silver ...

Tony   How much is that going to cost?

Elizabeth   I don't know exactly ...

Tony   You must have an idea ...

Elizabeth   It depends on numbers ... That's one of the things we have to discuss ...

Tony   How much is it going to cost?

Annie   We can discuss this later ...

Elizabeth (*taking a piece of paper from her handbag*)   For about two hundred ...

Tony *takes the estimate, which he dismisses immediately.*

Tony   I'm not paying that ...

Elizabeth   What...

Tony (*raising his voice*)   I'm not paying that...

Attention has turned to **Tony** *and* **Elizabeth**.

Elizabeth   But there are guests – important guests...

Nicholas   People from Central Office, you know, Tony...

Guy (*with a nod*)   Portillo...

Tony   Screw fucking Portillo – I'm not paying that!

Annie   Tony, please...

Pause.

The invitations are no big deal, Tony...

Nicholas   Is there a problem? – The vicar, you know...

Tony   What?

Nicholas   We were at school together...

Tony   You people always bloody are...

Nicholas   There's obviously something going on here...
Is Jacqui...

Tony   You leave her out of this! You bloody keep your dirty
hands off my Jacqui!

Elizabeth   Dad!

Annie   Tony...

Tony   It's all right for you – you're paying for the
honeymoon – You've bought the bloody restaurant.
Through an old mate, was it?

Nicholas   I've got no idea what's going on here but I think
you owe me an apology.

Pause.

Malcolm   Perhaps we should discuss things on another
day – When Christine gets back...

Amelia   Sounds like a good idea...

Annie   Tony?

Pause.

Tony (*quietly*)   I can't afford it ...

Pause.

Ursula   What?

Tony   I can't afford it ...

Elizabeth   We don't have to get those invitations ...

Tony   I can't afford the wedding! I haven't got a penny! D'you understand!

Elizabeth (*immediately fighting back the tears*)   What d'you mean? – What d'you mean?

Tony   I haven't got any money!

Elizabeth   The policies – insurance policies ...

Tony   There are no policies ...

Elizabeth   No ...

Ursula   But – what d'you mean you haven't got any money?

Tony   I'm completely broke ...

Pause.

I could only scrape together five grand ...

Elizabeth   It's not ...

Tony   And that's gone ...

Ursula   Where?

Tony   I went to a casino ... I thought I could ...

Annie   No!

Ursula   You bastard!

This unexpected outburst attracts everyone's attention.

I always wanted to be a bridesmaid – and now I never will be ...

She bursts into tears and exits.

Nicholas (*head in his hands*)   Christ . . .

Malcolm   Ursula . . .

Amelia   Leave her, Malcolm . . .

Elizabeth (*finding* **Annie**'s *arms*)   What am I going to do – everything's booked . . .

Annie   I know, darling . . .

Nicholas   Look here, if things are difficult, Christine and I . . .

Tony   I don't want your money!

Nicholas   But if . . . There are important people coming!

Tony   I want to pay for it! – I want to pay for it all!

Guy   Tony . . .

Tony   I want to pay for the dress, I want to pay for the church, I want to pay for the flowers, the photos, the video, the disco . . .

Elizabeth   I'm not having a disco – I'm having a string quartet . . .

Tony   I want to pay for the button-holes, the invitations, the cake, the hotel, I want to choose the hymns, and I want to watch them pull away in the car, with the string, and tin cans and confetti and know that I've paid for the damn lot, but I can't!

Pause. The sound is of **Elizabeth** *sobbing.*

Malcolm   Should I go and fetch some tea?

This is ignored. **Elizabeth** *pulls herself out of* **Annie**'s *arms and straightens herself.*

Elizabeth   Why are you doing this to me?

Annie   Lizzie . . .

Elizabeth   This is my wedding – the biggest day of my life . . . And you won't pay for it . . .

Annie   Elizabeth . . .

Elizabeth It's your family, isn't it? It's because they think you've gone off and left them now and you want to fit them back in by having a wedding they won't be jealous of . . .

Annie This isn't fair . . .

Elizabeth Well, we have left them! We're better than them and they can just rot in their stinking gutter for all I care!

Elizabeth *cries freely into her hands.*

Annie (*putting her arms around* **Elizabeth**)   She doesn't mean it, Tony . . .

Jacqui *enters. Everyone notices this. She wears an overcoat. Pause.*

Annie What's she doing here?

Tony I asked her to come . . .

Annie You asked her?

Tony I needed someone . . .

Annie You knew you were going to say this – to your daughter – and you asked her . . .

Jacqui I'll go . . .

Tony No . . .

Annie How dare you . . .

Tony She's my . . . I needed . . .

Annie And what about what Elizabeth needs!

Tony I'm sorry . . .

Annie It's too late for sorry!

Jacqui It's my fault – I shouldn't have come . . .

Annie You've taken away my husband from me and now you've taken away my daughter's wedding!

Tony That's not true – I did the money, I did it!

Long pause. **Joseph** *meanders into the room. He is very drunk and swigging from a can of lager.*

Amelia   Joseph . . .

Joseph   Right, Milly, all right, everyone . . .

Amelia   I thought you were gone . . .

Joseph   Tomorrow . . .

Annie   What are you doing, Joseph? – This isn't . . .

Joseph   I want to speak to you, Lizzie . . .

Amelia   No. Joseph –

Joseph   I want to speak to you . . .

Malcolm   Come on, Joe . . .

Joseph   I want to speak to you – Alone . . .

Nicholas   I don't think this is the time . . .

Joseph   When is the time? – That's what I want to know . . .

Elizabeth   I'll speak to you later . . .

Joseph (*lifting his can*)   Tomorrow I go up – in the sky . . .

Nicholas   Will you help me remove this young man, Guy?

Malcolm   Why don't you give me the can . . .

Joseph   I know . . .

Malcolm   You're going to spill it . . .

Joseph   I know what you all think of me . . .

Tony   Please, Joseph . . .

Malcolm (*reaching for the can*)   Give us that . . .

Joseph   You all think I'm an idiot . . .

Annie   You're making a fool of yourself . . .

Joseph   Well, I'm not . . .

Nicholas   Get ready to grab him, Guy . . . I'm giving you one chance, young man . . .

Joseph   Don't fucking young man me, you bowler-hatted bastard . . . (*He laughs, then shouts.*) I'm a man! You all hear that – I'm a man! Hear that, Lizzie – a man! More than bloody Henry ... (*He laughs.*)

Nicholas   You leave my boy ...

Joseph   He's useless – a complete arsehole – everybody knows it ...

Nicholas   I've a good mind to take you outside ...

Annie   Nicholas ...

Joseph   Why shouldn't I say it ... She doesn't love Henry ... She only wants him for the money ... Why can't you love me ... Look – Look ... I get on my knees ...

Malcolm *grabs the can.*

Tony   Get up, Joseph ...

Ursula *enters. She is soaking wet.*

Ursula   D'you know I've been in the garden – in the rain – crying ... Did anyone come and see if I was all right? Did you come and see if I was all right, Malcolm? You don't care about me – no one cares about me!

She turns and exits in tears.

Malcolm   Ursula! – Ursula ...

He follows **Ursula** *out.*

Joseph   Who rattled her cage?

Tony   Get up, Joseph ...

Joseph   No ...

Tony   Get up!

Joseph   You're all Tories – that's what it is – bloody Tories ...

Tony   Get up!

Joseph   I believe in the welfare state ...

Tony (*shaking* **Joseph** *violently*)   Get up, get up, get up!

Jacqui *moves over to* **Tony** *and takes him in her arms.* **Amelia** *moves over to* **Joseph**. **Nicholas** *looks at his bowler hat.*

Amelia   Come on, Joey – up you get . . .

Henry *enters, barely noticed at first. He too is soaking wet.*

Henry (*smiling broadly*)   Sorry I'm late – got shat on by a pigeon and I stopped to clean the pinstripe . . . (*A beat.*) I've been thinking about the menu for the wedding . . . How d'you fancy orange fool for pudding, Lizzy?

Elizabeth (*smiling broadly*)   I love you, Henry . . .

Elizabeth *finds her way into* **Henry**'s *arms.*

Scene Five

Late Saturday evening. An office in north London. **Tony** *stands alone in the darkened office illuminated only by the outside streetlight.*

Penny (*offstage*)   Who's in there? (*A beat.*) If that's you, Roger, you can just come out of there right now and clear your desk on Monday morning!

Pause. **Penny** *enters with a computer keyboard raised above her head as if to strike. She's wearing a quite sexy short dress, has obviously been out for the night and is a little drunk.* **Tony** *turns.*

Tony!

Tony   I'm sorry . . .

Penny   You nearly half-frightened me to death, you naughty boy!

Tony   I'm sorry . . .

Penny   What are you doing here this time of night? Have you been drinking? Are you drunk?

Tony *smiles and shakes his head.*

Tony   What are you doing here?

Penny   Oh – I've been out for dinner. I met this fantastic American drowning his sorrows in a bar round the corner –

and we got chatting. You'll never guess what, Tony – he's an oil baron! – and he took me to my favourite restaurant in Camden, and I said I'd show him where I work. He should be here in a second – He's just nipped to the twenty-four-hour garage to get some . . . Sugar – for the coffee –

Tony   There's plenty in the kitchen . . .

Penny   Is there? Silly me. Still, it's given us a moment to chat, eh, Tony? Are you all right?

Tony   I've just been thinking – I wanted somewhere quiet to think . . . I'll go if you like.

Penny   No, no, no, Tonny – you stay right there.

Pause.

Tony   You know – the things I've been thinking about this evening, Penny – all sorts of things. My life, my family, Jacqui, Elizabeth, what I want, what I'd like, what I need – all sorts of things – spinning round and round. I've been thinking about my childhood, growing up in the East End, and the journeys once or twice a year to Scotland to see my uncles. I used to watch my dad, and his two brothers year after year getting drunk round the table and promising that the next year I came up I'd be old enough to have a wee dram of whisky.

Pause.

I've thought about Jacqui – and Annie – and Elizabeth . . .

Pause.

Penny   Well, I hope I'm going to get an invite to her wedding – I've been very good to you, Tony . . .

Tony   You'll have to ask Nicholas – he's paying for the bloody thing.

Pause.

Penny   I love to hear you talk, Tony – In fact I was thinking now that Roger's gone . . .

Tony   What?

Penny   Now that Roger's gone . . .

Tony   Where?

Penny (*smiling*)   Oh – didn't you know? I gave him the push yesterday evening . . . I know he's your friend – but he just wasn't up to it at the end of the day . . .

Pause.

Well, I was thinking, Tony – You know, I know how you and Roger got on, and you'll miss him not being around to talk to in the office – about politics, and that sort of thing – and about how I'm not really up on that side of things as much as I should be. So . . . I've thought of just the trick. We could go on one of those weekends – I've got the brochure, Tony . . . Business and New Labour it's called – and it won't be such a steep learning curve with you there to show me the ropes – so to speak . . .

Tony   I should be going – Your American friend'll be here in a minute . . .

Penny   That doesn't matter – I'll tell him I've changed my mind . . .

Tony *goes to exit.* **Penny** *stops him, placing a hand on each of* **Tony***'s arms. Pause.* **Penny** *moves her hands gently up and down* **Tony***'s arms.*

Penny   What d'you think, Tony? I've had a look through the brochure and it's amazing – We'll definitely be able to work with them . . . Definitely.

Penny *raises a hand to brush* **Tony***'s cheek.* **Tony** *smiles, pulls* **Penny** *into his arms and they begin to kiss.*